Better Homes and Gardens®

easy
decorating
makeovers

Better Homes and Gardens® Books
Des Moines, Iowa

Better Homes and Gardens® Books
An imprint of Meredith® Books

Easy Decorating Makeovers

Editor: Vicki L. Ingham
Contributing Editors: Susan Andrews, Mary Baskin, Andrea Caughey, Deborah Hastings, Rebecca Jerdee, Catherine Kramer, Amy Muzzy Malin, Joetta Moulden, Wade Scherrer, Donna Talley Wendt, Linda Baltzell Wright
Art Director: Mick Schnepf
Copy Chief: Terri Fredrickson
Copy and Production Editor: Victoria Forlini
Editorial Operations Manager: Karen Schirm
Managers, Book Production: Pam Kvitne, Marjorie J. Schenkelberg
Contributing Copy Editor: Jane Woychick
Contributing Proofreaders: Becky Etchen, Julie Cahalan, Nancy Ruhling
Contributing Photographers: King Au/Studio Au, Fran Brennan, Ed Gohlich, Bob Greenspan, William Hopkins, Jenifer Jordan, Peter Krumhardt, Sylvia Martin, Emily Minton, Michael Partenio, Deborah Whitlaw
Illustrator: Michael Burns
Indexer: Sharon Duffy
Electronic Production Coordinator: Paula Forest
Editorial and Design Assistants: Kaye Chabot, Karen McFadden, Mary Lee Gavin

Meredith® Books
Editor in Chief: Linda Raglan Cunningham
Design Director: Matt Strelecki
Managing Editor: Gregory H. Kayko
Executive Editor, Home Decorating and Design: Denise L. Caringer

Publisher: James D. Blume
Executive Director, Marketing: Jeffrey Myers
Executive Director, New Business Development: Todd M. Davis
Executive Director, Sales: Ken Zagor

Director, Operations: George A. Susral
Director, Production: Douglas M. Johnston
Business Director: Jim Leonard

Vice President and General Manager: Douglas J. Guendel

Better Homes and Gardens® Magazine
Editor in Chief: Karol DeWulf Nickell

Meredith Publishing Group
President, Publishing Group: Stephen M. Lacy
Vice President-Publishing Director: Bob Mate

Meredith Corporation
Chairman and Chief Executive Officer: William T. Kerr

Chairman of the Executive Committee: E. T. Meredith III

Copyright© 2003 by Meredith Corporation, Des Moines, Iowa.
First Edition-3. All rights reserved. Printed in the United States of America.
Library of Congress Control Number: 2002109073
ISBN: 0-696-21722-8 soft cover; 0-696-21404-0 hard cover

All of us at Better Homes and Gardens® Books are dedicated to providing you with information and ideas to enhance your home. We welcome your comments and suggestions. Write to us at: Better Homes and Gardens Books, Home Decorating and Design Editorial Department, 1716 Locust St., Des Moines, IA 50309-3023.

If you would like to purchase any of our home decorating and design, cooking, crafts, gardening, or home improvement books, check wherever quality books are sold. Or visit us at: bhgbooks.com

Cover Photograph: King Au/Studio Au

3

✳ INTRODUCTION

My grandmother loved moving furniture around. It seemed like every time we went to visit, she had pulled the sofa, tables, and chairs into different positions. I think she felt that if a room stayed the same too long, it became stale. Changing it around made it feel new.

I don't change things as often as she did, but I do enjoy giving myself novel views from time to time—hanging paintings in varied combinations, creating new displays, and yes, rearranging the furniture. The satisfaction that comes from waking up tired rooms with a few simple changes is what inspired this book. We've photographed homes from around the country to illustrate creative and practical ways to revitalize your rooms. Many of the examples focus on using what you already have. Obviously that saves money and time, but more importantly, it makes your cherished furnishings and collections seem fresh.

Sometimes reviving your rooms requires more—a different color on the walls or a change of fabrics on furnishings and windows. Or you may need to make a few strategic purchases: A key piece of furniture or a new rug makes all the difference between a ho-hum room and one that sings. Let this book stir your creative juices—and then have fun transforming your rooms!

Vicki Ingham

Editor, *Easy Decorating Makeovers*

one.findafocus

When you walk into a room, what's the first thing you notice? The fireplace? A great view? An inviting sofa or an entertainment center? In a well-designed room, you'll instinctively recognize the linchpin, the element that holds everything together. This is the focal point, and every room needs one to feel comfortable and "right." A focal point gives the room a sense of order so you can find your place in it and feel at ease. If your room has a major architectural

feature, such as a fireplace or an expanse of windows overlooking beautiful scenery, you have a natural starting point for creating a focus. In rooms without such features, develop a focal point with a display of art or a key piece of furniture, such as an armoire in the living room or the bed in the bedroom. In a family room, the television (for better or for worse) is usually the center of interest, so it needs to be positioned where everyone can see it easily. To blend it into the room, partner it with a piece of furniture, such as an entertainment center or armoire, that has the presence to command attention. On the following pages, you'll see examples of how to make the most of focal points to bring rooms to life.

challenge

To emphasize the shape of the space in a room with a dramatic sloped ceiling and open plan. The all-white, unadorned walls actually disguise the lines of the room, and the black fireplace contrasts harshly with the white walls. The furniture arrangement, with a love seat angled across one corner and a sofa facing the fireplace, isn't as intimate as it could be for conversation, and whoever sits on the love seat misses out on a view of the fireplace. A red kilim rug warms the room with its color and texture, but the pattern is busy in this context.

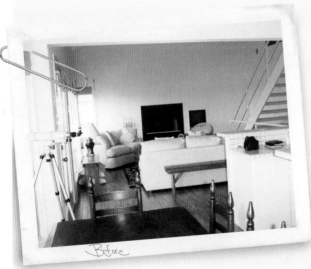

Above The far wall begs for artwork to tone down the black hole of the fireplace. The furniture arrangement also could be improved.

* solution

Install a grid of identically framed prints on the fireplace wall to enliven the space and create an arresting focal point. Rearrange the furniture for better balance and function.

theSPECIFICS

* **Emphasize the ceiling line** with a collection of prints hung to call attention to the shape of the space. Interior designer Sandy Lucas recommends planning the arrangement on paper, drawing the wall to scale to determine the best spacing. For this room she centered the first row of framed hunting prints 6 inches above the fireplace. She allowed 3 inches between each print. Before you begin hammering nails, lay out your arrangement on the floor to make sure it pleases you.

* **Focus the seating** on the fireplace by shifting the sofa and love seat into an L. Although this arrangement turns its back on the view of the outdoors, it concentrates on the inner space and the way the room is used—at night, for relaxing and conversation. It also leaves an

8

Above The kilim rug is too busy for this all-white room, and the furniture hangs off its edges.

Opposite A pattern-free sea-grass rug large enough to contain the seating pieces makes an uncluttered base for a more orderly furniture arrangement.

unobstructed path from the kitchen/dining area to the stairs. The new arrangement eliminates the need for two coffee tables, so the chest that sat in front of the love seat now settles beside the sofa. The plank coffee table serves both seating pieces. A pair of stools can serve as extra tables or chairs as needed.

✳ **Eliminate noisy pattern** by replacing the kilim rug with a neutral one made of sea grass. The new rug enhances the restful, beachside atmosphere and pulls the conversational grouping together.

✳ **Seek balance** by replacing the wicker chair with a heftier club chair. Angled at the corner, the chair accommodates family or guests when conversation is the main activity. When the family settles in to watch television, the club chair doesn't block the view.

✳ **Use large-scale objects as art.** A pair of antique doors hangs on the stair wall as art (see page 9), bringing texture and character to what would otherwise be a daunting blank space.

Above The bench holds a lamp, but the lamp is too far from the love seat for reading.

Left The sofa occupies this space more comfortably and focuses on the conversation area.

challenge

To bring personality to the eating area and kitchen of the beach house, in keeping with the look of the living room (see previous pages).

*solution

Add one focal-point object to bring the area to life.

theSPECIFICS

* **Fill the bare wall** at the end of the room with a cupboard. This functional piece adds lots of storage for dinnerware, and its handsome patina picks up the warm wood tones of the chairs and table, the kitchen barstool, and the matchstick blinds.

* **Emphasize height** by crowning the cupboard with a few objects to carry the eye to the ceiling. The basket and the bird sculpture have clean, simple shapes that harmonize with the lines of the crown molding and paneled doors on the cupboard.

* **Punctuate the space** above the windows. Hand-painted platters depicting Texas fish and shellfish add color and depth and urge the eye upward, expanding the sense of space.

Before

Above Good bones—plenty of tall windows and a pleasing and functional floor plan—create a light-filled space warmed by wood floors and an antique table and chairs. The room doesn't need much to feel lived in.

Opposite The cupboard immediately anchors the room and provides convenient storage for dinnerware and table linens.

Right Texas fish painted on plates by Houston artist Mary Thyssen suit the beach location, and the oblong shape contrasts with the geometry of the windows and furnishings.

12

challenge

To create a balanced room arrangement that takes advantage of the fireplace as the natural focal point. The wall-hugging arrangement focuses on the television, which isn't visually weighty enough to serve as an anchor. In addition, small objects along the mantel shelf and the prints above them form two dark parallel lines that don't relate to each other.

Above Positioning the recliner with its back to the room entrance seems to bar admission. With many objects of similar size placed close to the walls, the room has no clear focus.

Opposite An L-shape arrangement that opens to the breakfast area draws people in. Pulling the furniture away from the walls creates a cozier conversational grouping that conveys a warmer welcome than furniture pushed against the walls.

✳ solution

Pull seating pieces away from the wall into an L-shape grouping centered on the fireplace.

theSPECIFICS

✳ **Rearrange the seating pieces** to put the prettiest piece (a high-backed love seat) in a show-off position, so it's one of the first things visitors see when they enter the room. With the seating group opening toward the room entrance, the room feels more welcoming.

✳ **Pull the furniture in** from the walls to create a path behind the chairs and in front of the fireplace. The homeowners have two small children who also benefit from this new traffic path: It's much more interesting for crawling and playing than the large empty area of the previous arrangement.

✳ **Use tall plants** to tie the wall art to nearby furnishings. Connecting wall art to a reference point, such as the architecture or furnishings, integrates the artwork into the overall scheme.

✳ **Build a coffee table**, end tables, and an entertainment center

using modular cubes. As the young homeowners acquire more serious, permanent furnishings, the white cubes can move upstairs into a child's bedroom or into a home office.

✳Move the television to the windowed corner near the room entrance. In its new position, the television is out of sight from the entrance but easy to see from the seating group. Stylist Rebecca Jerdee built a temporary entertainment center out of white modular units, establishing a secondary focal point. An art light (a paper box) on top of the entertainment center gives the unit decorative interest.

✳Link the mantel to the prints above it with objects of varying heights. Candles provide the missing connection here, grouped with the tallest at the center. The small decorative objects that were lined up along the mantel can also be incorporated into the new display (see page 15). Instead of having no particular focus, they become part of a cohesive unit.

✳Employ strategic lighting to bring the room to life. In addition to general lighting from the windows and the overhead downlights, add task lighting (reading lamps near the chairs), decorative lighting (the paper box above the television), and accent lighting (an uplight on the floor to dramatize the plants). When the fireplace is in use and the candles are lit, kinetic, or active, light comes into play. Arrange light sources around the room so they form triangles; this provides balanced illumination.

Right The finest piece of furniture was tucked out of sight in a corner, while other seating lined the walls, leaving the area in front of the fireplace empty.

Opposite Laminate modular units create an entertainment center as well as a meandering coffee table that provides lots of storage and childproof surfaces.

17

challenge

To fit furnishings from a larger home into a new, smaller space. Pushing furniture against the wall to open up the center of the room is a common mistake in this situation. Instead of making the room feel more spacious, the arrangement throws the room out of balance and ignores the fireplace as the obvious focal point. In addition, the Windsor chair doesn't have enough visual weight to hold down its corner of the room, and the area rug is too small for the space.

Before

Above Everything tips out of balance when you ignore the natural focal point of a room. A too small rug in front of the sofa emphasizes the unfocused, lost-at-sea feeling of this space.

 # solution

Draw major seating pieces into an intimate grouping in front of the fireplace to create inviting comfort.

the SPECIFICS

* **Create instant intimacy** and focus by bringing the sofa into the room to face the fireplace. Interior arranger Kitty Starling advises looking at furnishings and accessories in terms of their shapes and considering how the shapes relate to each other and to the room. Then arrange them around the most prominent feature in the room.

* **Arrange for balance.** The wing chair stays put, now that it's comfortably balanced by the sofa. To soften the far corner of the room, Kitty brought in a folding screen. Paired with a Windsor chair, the screen balances the wing chair without making the room feel overstuffed. A table under the window also adds visual weight to hold down that side of the room. The ottoman was much too hefty for the Windsor chair, but in front of the fireplace, it's offset by the bench and sofa.

* **Replace the area rug** with a larger one in better scale with the room and the floor space.

❋Repurpose furnishings. The red bench takes center stage as a coffee table. The bench and the red rug pull out the warm hue in the sofa upholstery and in the accent pillow. The tole tray on a stand continues to do butler duty beside the sofa, but now it can be better seen and appreciated.

❋Play up the fireplace as the center of interest with an intriguing mantel display. Kitty added a few objects of different shapes and heights, placing the planter and plate in front of the painting to create depth. Allowing ivy to spill over the mantel's edge softens an otherwise hard line.

❋Position lamps in a triangle to create a balanced effect (it can be an acute triangle). Balanced lighting makes the room live better. If you have only two lamps, place them on a diagonal line rather than at each end of the sofa.

challenge

To give the playroom a cohesive look while defining different activity areas within it. The architecture helps define two areas, with the computer, sewing machine, and exercise equipment tucked into the bump-out at the front of the house. The openness of the space isn't necessarily a negative, but the different activities that go on here can result in visual clutter.

✳ solution

Use paint, a rug, and some furniture substitutions to define three activity areas in the large space. Add a folding screen to hide the exercise equipment when company comes.

the SPECIFICS

✳ **Define a "theater space"** by painting the television alcove black. Although this might seem daring, the color actually helps make the technical equipment disappear into the setback.

✳ **Layer an area rug** over the wall-to-wall carpeting to gather the seating into a well-defined conversational grouping.

✳ **Soften the window** without blocking the light by hanging simple flannel panels at the sides. The panels require no sewing; slits in the top edge receive the curtain rod.

✳ **Partition off the exercise area** in the far corner of the room (see the next page) with a folding screen made from bifold door panels from a home improvement center (see page 189 for instructions). When the homeowners want to work out, they can remove the screen to see the television.

✳ **Hang art low,** if the architecture permits, for

Before

Above The high contrast between the white walls and the dark entertainment center emphasizes the television as a large black box.

Opposite Painting the wall black absorbs the entertainment center and gives the room a dramatic, almost theatrical quality. A table replaces the little-used computer and sewing center in the far corner.

20

Above Pulling a narrow table away from the wall and up to the sofa puts it within reach for books and drinks and frees wall space for dramatically framed prints.

Opposite The folding screen (made from bifold door panels) makes a temporary wall when company comes, defining the boundary of the conversational grouping. A new area rug unifies the seating pieces. No-sew curtain panels and a valance cut from flannel soften the window without blocking natural light.

Before

22

Above The bookshelves need a little reorganizing to present a more orderly appearance.

Right Pairing baskets and boxes in the center of each shelf and flanking them with books and photo albums gives the eye a place to rest at each level. Pruning the collection of photos and objects allows those that remain to show up better.

unexpected drama and impact. Large pieces mounted on the low walls behind the sofa fall below eye level and make the ceiling seem higher.

✳ **Impose order on bookshelves** with baskets and boxes. Use them to organize magazines, CDs, and videocassettes. Arranged in the center of each shelf, pairs of baskets provide comfortably solid shapes to anchor tidy arrangements of photos, books, and collectibles.

Above A computer and sewing machine in the corner didn't get used as much in this room as they would elsewhere.

Left Stylist Linda Wright used inexpensive flannel to cover a glass-top table. For the topper, she indulged in a more expensive upholstery fabric—making a big impact for a small investment.

✱ Shuffle furnishings for function. Moving the sewing machine and computer to rooms where they are more likely to be used frees up the corner for a games table. Stylist Linda Wright skirted the table with black flannel, which is inexpensive and doesn't need hemming. The overskirt, which requires less yardage, is a more expensive upholstery fabric.

challenge

To emphasize the bed as the natural focal point of the room and to add punch with touches of pattern. Warm yellow walls with matching draperies give this bedroom a lovely golden warmth, but bare walls and plain bedding deprive the bed of the impact it deserves. In addition, the television is too heavy visually for its location.

✻ solution

Create a headboard effect on the wall behind the bed and add pattern with bedding to bring the room into focus.

theSPECIFICS

✻ **Build a bridge** between the horizontal of the bed and the vertical of the wall with art, architectural salvage, or textiles. Here, three old metal screen door inserts from a salvage yard are hung on the wall with nails. You also could use old shutters, a folding screen, a quilt, or large pressed-tin ceiling panels to achieve a

26

Before

similar effect. The treatment should be no wider than the bed but should be at least two-thirds the width of the bed. The height depends on the size of the bed. If you have a king- or queen-size platform, you may need to hang taller panels to balance the bed visually; shorter ones may look skimpy.

* **Dress the bed** in basic white—or your favorite solid color—and layer on pattern and complementary color with pillow shams and a quilt or spread. Interior designer Sally Dixon brought romantic pattern to the all-white bed with an antique quilt, comforter, and pillow shams. The florals introduce softness and a sense of luxury to the room.

* **Repurpose a pedestal table** originally intended for the living room to serve as a bedside table. It's a convenient height for books, alarm clock, and lamp, and the top offers plenty of space for photographs or favorite collectibles. For softly diffused light, choose a bedside lampshade in cream or taupe.

Above An end table that might ordinarily stand beside the sofa in the living room replaces the television and its stand in the bedroom.

Right Choose a bedside lamp that's tall enough to read by. Look for one with a three-way switch, or plug the lamp into a dimmer lamp control to give yourself lighting options.

Far right Choose accessories whose motifs and colors underscore decorating themes. Here, a floral vase echoes the bouquets on the pillow shams and comforter.

28

challenge

To play up the bed as the focal point and to create better balance in the furniture arrangement. With no art on the walls and no headboard to accent the bed, the room feels a little spartan, in spite of its sun-drenched Provençal color scheme.

solution

Emphasize the bed as the room's centerpiece with a do-it-yourself headboard.

theSPECIFICS

* **Make a headboard** using an accordion-style bamboo garden trellis from a garden shop or home center. Painted to look like antique bamboo (see page 176 for instructions), it adds pattern and texture to the wall and echoes the wood of the desk.
* **Place the slant-top desk flat** against the wall instead of angling it across the corner. This makes better use of wall space and provides a base for a casual display.
* **Add instant art** that requires no commitment (no nails in the wall) by propping a large square of pressed tin against the wall. The tin creates another level to move the eye around the space and serves as a background for potted plants that add life to the room.
* **Introduce color contrast** with a bed skirt that picks up the note of blue in the pillows. The blue skirt reinforces the pillows as a cooling counterpoint to the warm yellows in the room.
* **Move the chair** to the window to take advantage of natural light for reading. It's also in position for using at the desk when the drop front is opened.

Before

Above Angling the desk across the corner crowds the drapery and puts the desk out of balance with the bedside table. In addition, the little lamp on top is too small for the piece.

Opposite Moving the desk flat against the wall allows for the display of objects in better scale with the space. It also lets the drapery hang freely.

makeoverinanhour

The fireplace is a natural focal point, so the way
you dress the mantel can bring new spirit to the entire room. In an hour
or less, you can change the mantel display from ordinary to
extraordinary and capture a sense of the season.

fall

*You can choose to change everything on the mantel or leave one element that's a constant from season to season. Here, a favorite painting stays in place year-round, and the changing accessories bring out different colors in the artwork. For spring, plant ryegrass or wheat berries in terra-cotta pots of different sizes and shapes. The variety of shapes keeps the lineup from being rigid.

*Evoke summer with a few light-color items: Starfish, bleached-wood candlesticks, and a pale gray urn with a graceful fern offer a variety of shapes, textures, and heights to lead the eye along the mantel. A spare arrangement composed with casual asymmetry creates a

clean, uncluttered look that's psychologically cooling in summer's sticky weather.

* **For fall,** bring in warm wood tones, spice colors, and natural textures. Fill the urn with crafts foam and insert pheasant feathers (available from crafts stores) for a dramatic arrangement. Balance it with a pair of candlesticks and a large plate or bowl in tones of pumpkin and ocher.

* **For winter,** bring out your collectibles and showcase them on the mantel. Here, twig-stemmed trees stand high in the background, framing the painting. The arrangement of Santas along the shelf creates depth, and having at least one figure dangling its legs over the edge breaks the line of the mantel for a casual, playful look.

two.strikeabalance

Imagine yourself on a raft on the water with three friends. If all of you sit on the same side of the raft, you'll quickly be dunked as the raft tips over. To stay on an even keel, you have to distribute yourselves evenly, balancing the weight on each side. That same principle applies to room arranging, except that the weight you have to distribute is visual rather than physical. Balance in furniture arrangement and room design refers to a feeling of comfortable equilibrium in

the way furnishings relate to each other and to the space. The visual weight of objects is determined by their shape, size, and color. Proportion and scale enter the equation too. Proportion refers to the relationship between the size of a part and the whole. Scale is the size and shape of an object in relation to the space it occupies.

On another level, balance is also a lifestyle issue. Do the rooms in your house function well for your needs? If your house has a formal dining room that you never use, but you desperately need a home office or a playroom for children, bring your rooms into balance with your lifestyle by changing their designated functions to suit your requirements.

challenge

To give the entry wall more impact and a greater feeling of solidity. The furnishings are handsome antiques with light, graceful lines, but the table and chair seem too dainty and airy for the mirror and wall arrangements. In addition, the chair and urn tip the grouping to one side.

✳ solution

Bring furnishings with greater visual weight from elsewhere in the house to create a grouping that is compact and well-balanced.

theSPECIFICS

✳ **Create a powerful focus** by centering a chest or cupboard on the entry wall. Flank the chest with a pair of occasional chairs or extra dining chairs to define a triangle. For the peak of the triangle, interior arrangers Donna Mobley and Kitty Starling exchanged the mirror for a painting that had hung in the dining room. The painting introduces color and fills the wall space more completely than the mirror did.

✳ **Assemble accessories** in a variety of shapes and heights to form a still life that links the chest to the painting. A lamp raised on books for extra height sheds welcoming light and repeats (on a smaller scale) the vertical shape of the urn.

✳ **Punctuate the grouping** by raising the urn on a pedestal. Like an exclamation point, it finishes the decorating statement.

Above All the weight is up top, with large wall arrangements flanking the large mirror. Except for the lamp, no verticals link the table to the mirror.

Opposite Although the flower arrangement is centered, the objects on either side aren't mirror images of each other. The asymmetrical arrangement achieves balance because the objects have equivalent visual weight.

36

challenge

To eliminate the dueling focal points and find better balance for the furnishings. The fireplace is the natural focal point, but it's getting unwanted competition from the tall, mahogany-finish secretary. As a result, the whole room feels heavy on one side. The brown leather sofa doesn't harmonize with the yellow, blue, and white color scheme, and the Oriental rug is out of keeping with the light and airy palette.

✳ solution

Move the secretary to the adjacent wall. Replace the leather sofa with a slipcovered love seat and exchange the Oriental rug for a sisal one.

the SPECIFICS

✳ **Focus on the fireplace** by shifting the secretary to the adjacent wall. In its new position, the secretary provides a secondary focal point and also balances the china cabinet at the opposite end of the room (see page 41). Interior designer Sally Dixon lightened up the furniture grouping by replacing

Opposite In summer, the seating group edges toward the windowed corner to take advantage of the light. A sisal rug defines this room-within-a-room. In winter, chairs, love seat, and rug scoot toward the fireplace (see next page).

Before

38

the leather sofa with a white love seat that is in better proportion to the chairs. (Alternatively, the chairs could have been slipcovered in a darker fabric to bring them into harmony with the leather sofa.)

✳ **Regroup the seating pieces.** Frame the fireplace with the slipcovered chairs to create a relaxed symmetry. Position the largest seating piece, the love seat, opposite the fireplace instead of perpendicular to it; this creates a satisfying balance between two major features in the room.

✳ **Play up the mantel** by decorating it with matching pairs of objects placed on opposite sides of an imaginary centerline. This symmetry suits the formality of the traditional furnishings. The fireplace isn't centered between the windows, so to fill the extra wall space on the left side, Sally hung a pair of prints, aligning the top print with the top of the mantel picture. They're large enough to fill the space but light enough in color and visual weight not to detract from the mantel display.

✳ **Lighten the room** by replacing the Oriental rug with sisal. The neutral color and coarse, natural texture impart a breezier feeling than wool. And the rug helps pull the conversational grouping together.

✳ **Emphasize the color scheme** of yellow, blue, and white with new blue and white draperies. Although the original yellow draperies and undressed windows are a workable option, the new fabric repeats the blue and white of the slipcovers, creating a more unified feeling in the room.

Before

Left A room needs a clear focus to help orient you when you enter. Here, the secretary overshadows the architectural focal point, the fireplace. The room feels lopsided as a result.

challenge

To remedy the listing-ship feeling that results from clustering a chunky chair, ottoman, and sofa in one corner of the room. Placed parallel to the walls, the seating doesn't relate well to the focal point of the room, an entertainment center (not seen in the photos). The only piece of artwork hangs too high to connect to the furniture and seems small in proportion to the wall.

* solution

Place the sofa on the diagonal across the corner and replace the heavy chair and ottoman with lighter-weight canvas chairs. This arrangement brings the room into balance.

theSPECIFICS

* **Angle the rug and coffee table** too, paralleling the sofa. This creates a room-within-a-room and sets up a dynamic, active feeling. To balance that energy, arrange the furniture within the newly defined space symmetrically, placing like objects on opposite sides of an imaginary centerline: The butterfly chairs balance each other on each end of the coffee table, and the torchère balances the plant on a tall stand in front of the window.

* **Go for impact** with the artwork by choosing a larger framed print; hang it lower, so it connects visually to the sofa. Use art and accessories to lead the eye around the room, following a path of peaks and valleys. To create an interesting path, arrange items in overlapping triangles. The arrangement behind the sofa, for example, leads the eye from the high point of the lamp down to the silver platter and a pair of framed photos, defining a right triangle; the silver platter and photos make a skinny base for another triangle that includes the pair of stacked framed prints on the wall.

* **Use contrasts for interest.** Verticals, such as the torchère, table lamp, and plant stand, balance the horizontals of the coffee table and sofa. Round shapes, such as the silver platter, the vase of bear grass, and the smiling curves of the butterfly chairs, echo the rolled arms of the sofa and add a softening counterpoint to the squares and rectangles of furniture and framed pieces.

* **Rely on the power of color** to keep things in balance. The airy construction of the butterfly chairs makes them visual lightweights, but the bold, solid-color fabric allows them to stand up to the sofa's mass.

* **Suggest depth** by placing a tall plant stand beyond the sofa and in front of the windows. This draws the eye through the seating area toward the window. The raised plant also balances the tall torchère.

Before

Above Color has visual weight. The upholstered chair and ottoman may be smaller than the sofa, but the dark blue color makes them look heavier—and out of balance.

42

challenge

To redistribute the visual weight for a more comfortable rhythm. Dark, oversize sofa, chairs, and ottomans circle heavily around the large-screen television in the corner. When you enter the room, the first thing you see is this big black box. The glass-front bookcase seems squashed in the corner, while the angled bookcase behind the sofa is difficult to access. Sheer curtains admit light, but their barely there color blends with the walls, heightening the contrast with the dark furniture and keeping the room out of balance.

Above The angled bookcase behind the sofa is awkward to reach, and furniture and accessories are crowded in the far corner.

44

✳ solution

Move the entertainment center to the opposite corner and rearrange the furniture to create a better balanced, more welcoming arrangement.

theSPECIFICS

✳ **Angle the sofa** in front of the window. Now it faces the dining area and the entertainment center, which was moved to the opposite corner. Switching the glass-front bookcase to the corner behind the sofa balances the entertainment center and shows off the bookcase better. It also helps create a skyline effect, adding a vertical that mediates between the horizontal of the sofa and the vertical of the window.

✳ **Keep the club chairs** perpendicular to the sofa, but to relieve some of the weight at the center of the room, move one ottoman out to stand alone as a table (or extra seating). The dark upholstery tends to lower the center of gravity in the room; to provide lift, stylist Rebecca Jerdee added a tea table and nested book table in front of the sofa. The bleached wood also brings light into the center of the room, relieving the effect of all the dark leather.

✳ **Warm bare wood floors** with color and texture. A shaggy leather rug tosses a medium

tone on the floor, providing transition between the brown leather and the apricot walls.

✳ **Provide color balance** with medium-dark draperies and pillows. The simple drapery panels lift the eye, and the pattern adds a soft element to a rugged-feeling room. Floral and tweed pillows break up the expanses of leather and add comfort to the seating.

✳ **Use tall houseplants** to soften empty corners and balance tall furniture. A plant disk on wheels makes it easy to move the ficus tree and protects the wood floor from dampness.

✳ **Reorganize accessories** so they relate better to furnishings: Aim for variety without clutter. Instead of two framed maps, let one take center stage. The ship model, which was too large for its spot on the wall, receives more attention on a side table. The lamp and the globe stair-step the eye from the windows back down to the club chair.

challenge

To change room functions to suit the family's needs. Finding balance is a lifestyle issue here. The original layout of the house featured a living room, dining room, and large combination kitchen/family room. But what the new owners need is a playroom for a toddler and an infant where the parents can supervise them while doing other work.

✳ solution

Assess the layout and reassign room functions to meet the family's needs. The dining room becomes a playroom, and the kitchen/family room becomes a spacious kitchen/dining room (see page 48).

theSPECIFICS

* ✳ **Think location.** The former dining room is in the right spot to serve as a playroom—the kids are under constant supervision from adults in the living room, and parents in the kitchen can also easily check on the playroom. A colorful tent provides a fun focal point for the room, and there's space for the baby swing and other toys.
* ✳ **Hang colorful note cards** on a plastic chain to decorate the wall. As the children begin drawing and painting, add their artwork to the wall too.
* ✳ **Put up baby gates** when necessary to control traffic. A gate on the living room side protects good furniture and keeps art objects off-limits.

Above A wide opening joins the living room (previous page) and rarely used dining room. What the family needs is a playroom.

Opposite Toys create happy chaos in a room for kids. Grown-ups can keep an eye on them while watching television or working in the adjacent living room.

challenge

To make better use of the space in a kitchen/family room. The family room end isn't used for relaxing or socializing, so it ends up as a catchall area. With art hung high under a lofty cathedral ceiling, the space lacks intimacy, and the mantel display lacks cohesion.

✳solution

Turn the space into a dining room—it's large enough to accommodate the table fully extended. The children have their own table and chairs at one end.

theSPECIFICS

✳ **Move the sideboard** to stand below the large framed piece. The buffet fits comfortably in this spot, and it helps connect the artwork to the room. Ideally, the framed piece should hang lower to relate to the mantel and furniture, but when this isn't possible, use tall items to forge a visual link.

✳ **Center the table** in the remaining space. The table is now the axis of the room, so align the framed photographs on the mantel with it rather than with the fireplace opening.

✳ **Create better balance** on the mantel with a simpler grouping of objects. Resting the framed pieces on the mantel keeps the focus low, on the living space.

Above A large print floats high on the wall, disconnected from the setting. Above the mantel, the framed pieces are spaced too far apart, and small objects clutter the mantel.

Right: A simpler mantel display emphasizes the table as the room's axis, rather than the fireplace. Although the "rules" dictate using odd numbers of objects, varying the shapes and heights of the pitchers relaxes this foursome so the display isn't stiff.

challenge

To lighten and refresh a 1958 ranch house with color and to rearrange furnishings for better balance and function. The furniture hugs the walls in the living room; the pieces are out of scale with the space and with each other, and the mix of styles is not successful. Two main walls in the living area are brown wood paneling; this, along with the avocado-green wall-to-wall carpeting, makes the house feel dark and dated. In the dining room, the table and chairs float in the middle of a large space.

✳solution

Paint the walls and change the flooring. Then arrange furniture in new, more intimate groupings, adding a few pieces that are in better scale with the major upholstered ones.

theSPECIFICS

✳ **Start with color for punch.** Because the homeowner collects midcentury modern furniture and accessories and loved the extra-long sofa, designer Susan Andrews chose greenish gold, chocolate, and red for the new color scheme. These hues are rooted in the 1950s but still have a contemporary edge. The paneling is painted greenish

Above The TV stand is too wimpy to stand up to the muscular armchairs and large television.

Right An armoire now hides the television and anchors one corner of the new seating group. A pair of new wooden armchairs defines this room-within-a-room.

50

Inset The skirted table is too high for the sofa, too big for the lamp, and too small for the wooden armchair.

Below Tables with stainless-steel tops tuck into the corners beside the sofa. They're the right height for the seating, and the vintage lamps are a better shape and size for the tables and the space.

Before

Above The chair and ottoman have a pleasingly comfortable appearance, but the chair's vertical profile and the ground-hugging shapes of both pieces make them look too heavy.

Right A lower profile, boxy shapes, and slender legs give this chair and ottoman a lighter look. The vintage 1950s floor lamp adds needed light. The bookcase-on-wheels rolls over to stand in front of the window, where it balances the new armoire on the other side of the room.

gold, and the tongue-and-groove paneled ceiling and beams are painted light-reflecting white.

✳ **Rip up the carpet.** If time and budget don't allow for hardwood floors to be installed, try a hardboard product (such as Masonite), which is brown and comes in 4×8-foot sheets with a beveled edge. Glue the sheets directly to the subflooring, using a polymer adhesive (such as Liquid Nails); then apply three coats of polyurethane with a large paint pad. The results look like stained concrete that has been scored, so it's clean and contemporary, yet warm. It's also economical: Covering the entire living and dining area cost only $200.

✳ **Freshen the brick fireplace** with paint. Susan chose a warm red that works with the colors in the living room as well as in the dining room.

✳ **Break up the long living room** by creating spaces within the space. The long sofa moved from in front of the windows to the end wall, where it anchors a conversational grouping (see page 51). The upholstered red armchairs frame it at each end, and a pair of new wooden armchairs faces the sofa across an ebony Nelson bench that serves as a coffee table. This grouping is now the first thing

you see when you come into the room, and it provides an inviting destination that draws visitors in.

✳ **Use oversize, solid-color pillows** to help minimize the sofa's length and to add comfort and color accents.

✳ **Replace the tables and lamps,** which are out of scale with the upholstered pieces. The new ones are low enough for the sofa but high enough for the armchairs.

Before

Above The collection of vintage clocks has more impact now, thanks to brighter color on the paneling. A vintage arrow-shape sign makes a striking sculpture.

Left At one point, the homeowner tried the armchair and skirted table against the paneled wall beside the television, but the scale and proportions still didn't feel right.

53

* **Paint the dining room** for dramatic warmth. This room is used primarily in the evening, and the contrast between white upholstered chairs and darker walls is stunning.

* **Center the table and chairs** in the room. Before, they were close to the fireplace, leaving the rest of the room empty. The same sisal rug anchors the pieces. Susan had an electrician adjust the track lighting to accommodate vintage dropped lights.

* **Give the eye a destination.** A large painting on the end wall supplies the

Before

Inset With the dining table and chairs pulled toward the fireplace, the parsons-table sideboard seems like an afterthought, and half the room stands empty.

Centering the dining table in the room gives the sideboard new purpose as a secondary focal point. Geometric shapes and blocks of color repeating around the room unify the space.

55

view and underscores the retro theme. Use furniture as sculpture too: The friendly shape of a Hans Wegner chair shows up crisply against the deep green-gold of the wall.

✳ **Create a secondary focal point.** Over the sideboard, Susan hung another large-scale painting (see page 54). Keeping accessories clean and bold creates quiet drama here.

✳ **Add a conversation spot.** A pair of new chairs make up a fireside seating area that balances the placement of the dining table. Susan chose a contemporary chair design with a muted retro pattern that repeats the color scheme. Then she married them with a vintage lamp, table, and clock for a seamlessly harmonious look.

✳ **Use collectibles for personality.** The homeowner's collection of mid-20th-century clocks hangs on the walls in the living room and dining room. The clocks show up much better than before, however, now that the paneling is green-gold and the brick is a brighter red-orange.

✳ **Repeat color for balance.** Bright, dark, or high-contrast colors appear heavier than pale or neutral hues. When the strongest color is on the wall, repeat the color in accessories or furnishings. The red-orange fireplace and upholstered armchairs could dominate the dining room in terms of visual weight, but accents of red in the light fixtures and in the art at the other end of the room bring the color into balance.

✳ **Draw on the power of pattern.** Large or bold patterns look weightier and more substantial than dainty designs

or solid colors. The chairs near the fireplace have modest proportions, but the bold pattern makes them substantial enough to stand up to the massive brick fireplace.

✳ **Play with shape.** Simple shapes and clean lines appear lighter in weight than exaggerated or unusual shapes. Leggy, straight-back chairs upholstered in white make good lightweight partners for the glass dining table (see page 55). A boxy chair and ottoman (see page 52) sit more lightly in the living room than the old gray chair and ottoman, which had a hefty look.

Opposite A couple of chairs, a table, and a lamp give this end of the dining room a cozy new function. Treating the fireplace as a wall worthy of art emphasizes the feeling of a mini-room. Tap a small nail into the mortar joint to hang lightweight art and collectibles on brick.

Below A snapshot of the work in progress shows the dropped lights and the shifted table, but the remaining improvements have yet to be made.

Before

challenge

To alleviate the cramped feeling in a small living room. Window treatments installed below the upper set of windows ruin the overall proportions of the windows and make the ceiling seem lower. In addition, the furniture arrangement circles around the center of the room and lacks intimacy.

✳solution

Raising the window treatments instantly enlarges the sense of space and refocuses attention on the graceful proportions of the windows. Rearranging the furniture establishes comfortable balance.

theSPECIFICS

✳ **Remount the swag** and jabots above the top of the upper windows. The fabric now softens the architecture without detracting from it.

✳ **Bring the seating pieces** to order. Align the coffee table with the fireplace. This emphasizes the fireplace as the room's focal point and creates an axis for lining up seating. The sofa (not seen in the Before photo) changes places with the entertainment center (just visible beside the window). Now when guests enter the room, they see the seating and fireplace first, and the room has a more welcoming feeling.

✳ **Strengthen the color scheme** by moving the red ottoman to another room. Although the piece picks up the color in the painting, there's not enough red in the room to integrate the ottoman into the color scheme.

Before

Opposite Squaring up the upholstered armchairs to face the sofa across the coffee table brings a feeling of quiet order to the room. On the mantel, candlesticks link the large painting to the mantel shelf.

DECORATING STEP-BY-STEP

Balance a major furniture piece and create a secondary focal point using a collage of wall art.

artfulDISPLAY

* **Create a collage** for flexibility—it's easy to change items from time to time for a new look.

* **Limit the number of objects** in the collage and arrange them in an irregular pattern (as shown opposite) for a contemporary look. If you prefer a traditional approach that covers the wall more densely, choose objects that are all the same color; this provides impact without creating chaotic clutter.

* **Add dimension** to the display with items that project from the wall into the space of the room. Brackets, architectural salvage, or wall sculpture add interest by keeping the collage from feeling too flat.

theSPECIFICS

step 1. Center the largest piece over the sofa. Flanked by a chest of drawers and a low table, the sofa is the axis for the wall display. Molding divides the wall into four panels, which guide the placement of objects. To create a similar effect on unpaneled walls, use the edges of furniture to suggest imaginary vertical lines that divide the wall space into sections.

step 2. Add lamps on the end tables. Besides washing the wall with cones of illumination, the lamps introduce verticals that lead the eye upward toward the wall display.

step 3. Install brackets on each side of the center picture for three-dimensional interest. Rest objects of different sizes and shapes on the brackets for a more interesting composition. Hang a medium-size item, such as an ornate empty frame, high in the left panel to carry the eye to the ceiling.

step 4. Define the outside edge of the display with a vertical; otherwise it will feel too loose and open-ended.

Below left Without some clever arranging on the opposite side of the room, this beautiful armoire could have tipped the scale.

A combination of antique and new seating pieces, lamps, and art on the wall provides enough variety in shape, line, and texture to equalize the room.

61

step 1.

Aligning the sofa with one paneled section allows you to create a balanced composition over the sofa, using the paneled areas as guides. Center the largest framed piece above the sofa, hanging it low enough to relate to the furniture.

step 2.

Add a lamp at each end of the sofa. They can be different styles and heights and still create formal balance if the shades align at about the same level.

62

step 3.

Hang a pair of brackets on either side of the framed piece, placing them so they're at about the height of the lampshades but not precisely aligned with them. To avoid stodgy symmetry, prop a photograph or painting on one bracket and a stone ball or vase on the other. Varying the size and shape of the items makes a more interesting composition. Fill out the left panel and carry the eye to the ceiling with an ornate, empty frame. Crown the central framed piece with a plaque to serve as punctuation.

step 4.

Add a pair of paintings in matching frames above the chest, aligning the outside edges with the edge of the chest. These frames define the boundary of the grouping and add vertical emphasis, repeating the vertical lines of the molded paneling on the walls.

before

makeover in

Don't Hang 'em high: Anchor artwork to the furniture for a feeling of comfortable balance.

It's a common mistake to hang wall art too high so that it doesn't relate to nearby furnishings or to the architecture. This isolation makes the art look random and spotty, and the room feels oddly out of joint. **Remedy the imbalance** by lowering the art so that it's 4 to 6 inches above a table or chest; place it at seated eye level if it's adjacent to a chair or sofa.

Use accessories to bridge the gap. Look through cupboards and closets for objects whose size, shape, and color will complement the colors in the artwork. Candlesticks, vases, and pitchers are obvious choices for verticals that will link the tabletop to the framed piece, but you can also use smaller framed pieces, sculpture, or

bowls and raise them on stacks of books. In the photo opposite above, rusted metal cans and a rusted-look picture frame harmonize with the warm neutrals of the black and white photographs and the dark brown table. The tall, slender cans lead the eye from the tabletop up to the photos, and the flowers add graceful shapes and lines, lifting the eye still higher. The footed picture frame injects variety with a different shape. It's not quite tall enough, so standing it on a book raises it to overlap the wall art by about an inch to make the needed connection.

For hallways or any area where you're most likely to view the art from a standing position, hang the pieces so they're at eye level from that position. If you and your housemates have very different eye levels, split the difference to find a comfortable compromise.

after

Below When you hang pictures over a sofa, plan for the display to be about two-thirds the width of the sofa and about 6 inches above the sofa's back. If you're using several pieces, consider following the contour of the sofa back for a more interesting line.

Below Dare to hang pictures lower than you might think you should. Sandwiching this art photograph between the lampshade and the tabletop puts it at an intimate, seated eye level. The framed piece on the stack of books leads the eye directly to the photo.

Below Create a focal point by balancing one large piece with two smaller ones. Hang the pieces close together so the frames align (or nearly do) to allow the group to work as a unit. Prop a fourth piece against the poster to link the grouping to the bookcase.

65

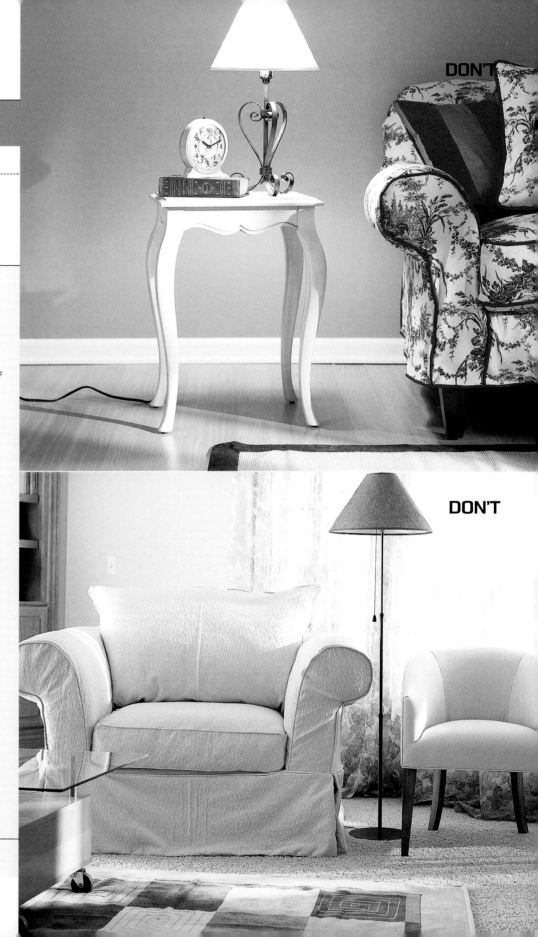

WHAT'S WRONG WITH THIS PICTURE?

HAPPY PAIRINGS

Opposites may attract in life, but in furniture arranging, a perfect marriage depends on similarity of size and scale. If you like chunky oversize sofas and chairs, pair them with sturdy tables and lamps that have solid, stable shapes. If you prefer slim, leggy chairs, choose side tables that are similarly slender. To avoid the "forest of legs" effect, however, consider a coffee table that carries its weight low (see the photo below right) but is in scale with the chairs. When you're assessing the visual weight of a chair or sofa, consider its shape, height, and width. An unusual or eye-catching shape, such as rolled arms or exaggerated curves, can make a chair or sofa look heavier than a piece with simple lines. A chair or sofa with a skirt also looks heavier than one with bare legs.

DON'T

DON'T

DO

Opposite Although it's the right height, this side table is too leggy and dainty to partner with the chunky slipcovered sofa.

Left A small chest whose top is slightly higher than the arm of the sofa is a much better match because its visual weight balances that of the sofa.

DO

Opposite Each of these pieces is attractive, but they don't belong in the same room. The rolled-arm chair is much too massive in comparison to the shorter, smaller, leggier chair beside it.

Left Choose sofas and chairs with backs that are about the same height. They should vary by no more than 6 inches. If there's too much difference in the heights, your eye will bounce around the room, making you feel seasick.

68

three.changethesenseofspace

If your room is feeling a little cramped, try rearranging your furniture. You may be surprised to find that furniture placement significantly changes the way your space feels and functions. Thoughtful positioning of seating, tables, and accessories can expand the apparent size of a small or boxy space or shrink a large room to give it intimacy and human scale. Making rooms function better

by using space more effectively is one of the primary jobs of interior arrangers, a relatively new breed of interior decorator. Practitioners specialize in using what you already have in your home, displaying and organizing furnishings and accessories according to basic design principles. You'll see examples of their work on the pages that follow. Apply their tips and ideas to your own rooms, or to find interior arrangers in your area, check out their professional association's website at www.interiorarrangement.org.

challenge

To make an ordinary boxy dining room and living room feel extraordinary. In the dining room, the predictable table arrangement parallel to the walls allows the strong wall color to become almost overpowering. The room could also use accessories to make it more appealing, both for entertaining and for everyday enjoyment.

✳solution

Place furnishings on the diagonal to open up the space and add visual excitement.

thespecifics

✳ **Use the dining table for display.** When you're not dining, treat the surface like any tabletop in your home—as an opportunity to create a pleasing composition. Interior arrangers Lisa Billings and Susie Ingram used fabric, tassels, stars, and globes to create a still life that combines shiny, dull, and nubbly textures.

✳ **Pay attention to the corners.** The table leads your eye to a corner, so put something spectacular there to warrant the attention. Floor candlestands with tall pillars and a vase of curly willow on a pedestal work like exclamation points. For special occasions, enhance the arrangement with fresh fruit and flowers. To balance the verticals and soften the adjacent corner, install a large, rounded plant there.

✳ **Anchor the table** with a rug. The rug should be large enough to contain the table and chairs, with room for chairs to be pushed back from the table. Lay the rug parallel to the table to preserve a well-ordered look. A

Before

Above Strong color creates drama in the dining room, but the predictable furniture placement doesn't offer matching excitement.

Opposite Angling the table and anchoring it with a rug on the same diagonal produces a livelier look. Plain burlap shades warm up the windows without hiding the handsome woodwork.

70

jute rug adds texture and warmth without introducing additional color that could make the room feel dark and heavy.

* **Repeat diagonals** in the adjoining living room. Diagonals make a longer line for the eye to follow across the room and so expand the sense of space. Angling the sofa also opens up the seating group, drawing in visitors.

* **Balance the movement** by leaving the coffee table in its original position, squared up to the fireplace. This keeps you from feeling funneled into a vortex; it also emphasizes the fireplace as the focal point.

* **Unify the seating group** with an area rug. If the rug is big enough to tuck under the seating, it creates a more expansive effect and keeps the furniture from appearing to float in the space.

* **Wake up a dull corner** by moving the artwork from the mantel to join the print already on the wall. A floor lamp with a red shade adds a burst of color by day and warm light by night.

* **Give the mantel drama** by using objects in scale with the architecture. Resting a tall

mirror and framed print on the mantel instead of hanging them conveys a casual look and lets you change displays without making more nail holes in the wall. Hanging one small piece has an unexpectedly intimate effect—it draws you closer, and like the period at the end of a sentence, it completes the arrangement.

* **Express your interests** with a display of favorite objects on the coffee table. Choose items that appeal to you because of their color, texture, or shape. Interior arrangers emphasize that it's important to have something tall on the coffee table, such as the candlesticks, so that you have a visual lift in the center of the room.

* **Show off your best furniture** by positioning it where it can be

Before

seen and appreciated. An Empire-style chest of drawers went unnoticed on a short wall (not shown) but became a secondary focal point when moved to the adjacent wall (see below). Pair it with artwork and arrange accessories on the chest to overlap the wall art, creating a visual link. Use tall plants as vertical accents in otherwise dead corners.

Left Make the most of corners by treating them as secondary focal points. The framed piece is wider than the chest, so drawing up a side chair helps balance the size of the painting.

Opposite The visual weight of the furniture hugs the floor and keeps the focus low. To lift the eye, use vertical elements, such as floor lamps, candlesticks, or plants, in corners and in the middle of the room.

challenge

To enlarge the sense of space in a narrow enclosed porch. The room benefits from a wall of glass doors and windows on one side and a wide cased opening on the other, connecting the porch to the living room (not shown). But within the room itself, the furnishings feel a bit crowded, and wall displays could be more effectively arranged.

✳ solution

Pull the seating pieces into the room to relieve the crowded feeling and enhance the sense of space. This also opens up room for displays and better use of lighting.

thespecifics

✳ **Pull seating away from walls.** Even in a narrow room, this enhances the sense of space because it creates depth. Interior arrangers Donna Mobley and Kitty Starling tucked a small table behind the sofa to provide a spot for a lamp, one of three that now illuminate the room with cozy pools of light. To distribute light evenly around the room and avoid shadowy spots, use at least three lamps placed in a triangle. Also vary the heights of the lamps so the light is cast at different levels.

✳ **Lift the eye** with dramatic verticals. This is another trick for increasing the perceived space in a room. Pulling the sofa forward opened space in the corner for Donna to stack the two end tables to form a column. This becomes a stage for a display that incorporates

Before

Above Your first instinct in a small room is to push the furniture against the wall, but that squeezes the side table into the corner. The framed watercolor and the baskets of ferns hang too high and don't relate to one other effectively.

Opposite Moving the sofa into the room relieves crowding. Using accessories to create dramatic verticals enhances the illusion of space.

74

Above Verticals—lamps, flowers, wall baskets—lift the eye and create an impression of expansive space even in a small room.

Before

Above Lining up the chairs along the window wall creates an awkward conversational grouping. The television looks like an afterthought standing on a low wicker basket.

objects of different sizes and shapes. "I tell people to go overscale for impact," says Donna.

✳ **Create a focal point.** The lamp and stacked tables frame the wall behind the sofa, so Donna and Kitty filled the space with more verticals—a print and a tole container with dried leaves urge the eye toward the ceiling, emphasizing a lofty sense of space. "You want to go up into the space to make a statement," says Kitty. Tall flowers on the coffee table perform the same function.

✳ **Match accessories to the space.** The fern-filled cone-shape baskets hanging above the sofa were too small for the space and were too far apart to relate well to each other. Donna moved them to the opposite wall, beside the door to the breakfast area. Here they form a column that suits the proportions of the wall. A small painted chest from elsewhere in the house moves into the corner to provide handy storage and a visual base for the baskets.

✳ **Use large-scale pieces for balance.** A baker's rack from the breakfast area makes a better television stand than the wicker storage basket because it's large enough to anchor the corner and balance the sofa. Angled across the corner, the unit fits into the room without crowding, and the top shelf provides a spot for another lamp at a different level.

✳ **Unify the conversation area** with a rug. Its green color picks up the green element in the cushion fabric and adds warmth to the terra-cotta floor.

✳ **Add color accents.** Donna found a set of sunflower plates tucked away in a cabinet and lined them up above the windows. Here they reinforce the colors in the fabric and walls, strengthening the room's color scheme. They also take the eye to the ceiling, enlarging the sense of space.

challenge

To redefine spaces in an open living/dining room to give each area its own identity and function. Although the options for arranging furniture in the dining room are somewhat limited, the living area (see page 80) is more flexible. The challenge is to find the best arrangement for entertaining a small group in a formal but comfortable setting.

✱ solution

In the dining room, transferring the secondary focus from the side wall to the corner makes the room feel solidly anchored. In the living room (see page 80), the sofa creates a wall that encloses a cozy conversation area. Large Oriental rugs stay where they were to define the two areas; the hardwood floor makes a path between them.

theSPECIFICS

✱ **Create a new focal point** in the dining room. The sideboard and painting are handsome, but for more drama and greater visual weight, interior arrangers Donna Mobley and Kitty Starling brought in a beautiful antique corner cupboard from the bedroom. The piece fills the corner with a commanding presence and offers a place to showcase china and silver.

✱ **Showcase special pieces** on the table itself. Display a tureen and its lid as if they were art objects, for example, and fill the tureen with greenery and flowers from the garden. This gives you something pretty to look at in the dining room even when you're not entertaining.

Before

Above This standard dining room arrangement is functional and attractive, but for a change, move a cupboard into the corner.

Opposite To make your corner cupboard both useful and beautiful, arrange the contents with attention to variety in shapes, heights, and sizes. For example, lay some goblets on their sides to create a more interesting line.

Using the sofa as a divider defines the living area as its own space. On the end wall, replacing the tall mahogany cupboard with a golden pine chest and gilt-frame mirror gives the eye a lighter-toned destination.

* **Reposition living room** furniture. Turning the sofa to face the windows encloses the living room and gives it a more intimate feeling. To create a fourth "wall," Kitty and Donna moved a desk from the entry to the living room. They also grouped the tall side table and upholstered armchairs in one corner. This completes the

Before

conversational grouping and balances the desk. A side chair pulled up to the desk offers a useful spot for writing notes or reading mail—and supplies extra seating in the living room.

* **Link the two areas** with a secondary focal point. Although a tall cupboard did the job in the old arrangement, it seemed too dark and heavy once the sofa was moved. Now a low, honey-colored chest and gilt-frame mirror fill the space. Because they are lighter in color, they can hold down the end of the room without looking overweight.

* **Play with accessories** to compose pleasing displays that link tabletops to the walls behind them. Look at objects in

terms of their shapes, colors, and textures; combine and position them so they lead your eye along a continuous path. Below, for example, a vase on its side forms a line that curves from the tabletop to a framed print, which then carries the eye to the lamp. Use stacks of books for height if necessary to achieve a variety of levels. On the wall, a bracketed shelf showcases a porcelain plate. In drawing attention beyond the lamp and tabletop display, the wall decoration suggests a sense of depth. Blank space is important too—leaving the adjacent corner wall undecorated enhances the impact of its neighbor.

Below Partnering the upholstered armchairs with a tall, square table creates a grouping that's visually weighty enough to balance the sofa. The table lamp, raised on books, fills the corner with a strong vertical element.

challenge

To make better use of space in a long, large room. At one end, heavy leather furniture and upholstered pieces gather around an armoire that holds the television. The other half of the room is unfurnished except for an airy looking table and metal garden chairs drawn up to the sliding glass doors. Area rugs float like islands on the open floor space.

✳ solution

Rearrange furniture to define two living areas that use the space better. Add secondary focal points at the formerly unused end to balance the seating group. Swap furniture between the sunroom and the adjacent family room to introduce a lighter look.

thespecifics

✳ **Use the floor space.** You might think that leaving the middle of a large room empty of furniture would create openness, but it actually promotes a cavernous feeling. As a remedy, move the table and chairs from the side into the middle of one half of the room to balance the seating group at the other end. Room arrangers Donna Mobley and Kitty Starling angled the table on a diagonally placed dhurrie rug for a more dynamic feeling that helps draw people into the room. "If you walk into a room with all of the furniture pushed against the walls," says Kitty, "you don't feel drawn in. You want to live in your space, not around the perimeter."

✳ **Fill the corners.** A skirted table and wicker chair turn an empty corner into a spot for reading or bird-watching. At the other end

Before

Above With most of the furniture clustered at one end, the rest of the sunroom feels underfurnished and underused.

Opposite A skirted table fills a formerly empty corner with a block of color. A lamp, artwork, and a chair create an inviting vignette.

of the room, a sculptural plant softens the corner and provides a high point in the "city skyline" effect that room arrangers aim to establish. "You want to create peaks and valleys throughout the room," says Donna. "All horizontal lines or all verticals will be boring."

✳ **Try on a theme.** A theme or motif can harmonize furnishings with the architecture and stamp the room with personality. In this sunroom, the abundance of light and the hand-painted armoire suggested an island or tropical look, so the decorators brought in a rattan love seat and chairs from the adjacent family room (not shown). A light-colored dhurrie rug replaces the wool Oriental, which moved to the family room. (The leather and upholstered pieces are also much more at home in that cozier wintertime space.)

✳ **Create interesting nooks.** In the empty wall space beside the armoire, Kitty and Donna installed a Chinese table and wicker chair. The table, displaying a lamp and a plant, serves as a desk and a secondary focus. According to the room arrangers, plants and lamps are key to sculpting space and breathing life into a room. Placing these elements to define triangles around the room ensures good balance.

✳ **Anchor art to something nearby.** "When we hang art," says Donna, "we align it with the top or bottom of an adjacent lampshade or with a mullion in the window or with the inside frame of the window. It should align with or center on some nearby feature so it relates logically to the room." She also advises leaving

Above Overstuffed leather and upholstered seating pieces seem too wintry for this light-filled space.

Opposite Rattan furniture (which had been in the adjacent family room) better suits the beachy, island feeling of the architecture and the landscape outside.

enough space between items in a grouping so they fill the wall space. If you bunch them too close together, they'll seem to huddle forlornly in a vast expanse of wall.

✳ **Express yourself with accessories.** Any surface—coffee table, chest, buffet, or side table—offers a platform for presenting objects that reflect your interests or please your eye. "The accessories tell your story," says Donna. There should always be something to make you smile too, she adds. That's why she gave a large pottery frog a place of honor on the coffee table and plopped a straw hat on its head.

✳ **Establish secondary focal points.** To fill a formerly empty spot at the back of the room, Donna and Kitty brought in the sideboard from the dining room (see page 78) and placed it on the wall adjacent to the kitchen (see page 87). The sideboard provides welcome

85

Before

Above The wall beside the kitchen plays host to a lonely plant and a painting that floats disconnected from any furnishings or architectural feature.

Left Placing something tall on the coffee table provides lift in the middle of the room. A vase in a tripod holder is dramatic for special occasions, but when it's time to watch television, the tripod moves to the floor beside the armoire. A table next to the armoire fills a once empty wall with new purpose, offering additional seating for conversation.

visual weight and another stage for a creative, themed display. Here the room arrangers brought together two paintings that had been hanging separately elsewhere, a lamp from another room (the pineapple base suited the island decorating theme), seashells from the family room bookshelves, and a bright yellow radio they found in a cupboard. In a large space, Kitty says, it's best to use larger-scale accessories; lots of little objects can look fussy.

A sideboard provides useful storage space as well as a surface for display. It also anchors the wall art, linking it to the room's furnishings. The lamp and flowerpot stretch up into the space occupied by the paintings, tying the horizontal surface of the sideboard to the vertical of the wall. When you're creating tabletop displays with a wall as background, always include verticals that overlap the wall art to knit the horizontal and vertical surfaces together.

challenge

To enlarge the sense of space in a boxy kitchen/breakfast area and to improve the feeling of flow in an open-plan townhouse. Floral wallpaper above the chair rail and a dark wallcovering as a wainscot chop up the kitchen and make it feel cluttered and busy. In addition, the open-plan house incorporates three types of flooring—linoleum, tile, and carpet—in a relatively small area. Even though neutral color unifies the three materials, the different textures break up the space, emphasizing three separate zones: kitchen, entry, and dining room.

✱ solution

For the two wallpapers substitute a single, airy pattern to enhance the sense of space. Replace the three flooring types in the kitchen, entry, and dining room with a single material.

thespecifics

✱ **Eliminate visual clutter** by keeping pattern to a minimum and creating a focal point. The pale blue toile wallpaper is softer and airier than the old wallcovering, giving the walls interest while allowing the room to breathe. An open-shelf cupboard offers the eye a place to rest and adds needed height, making the space feel larger. Its crackled finish blends with the country style of the new breakfast table and chairs. Displaying solid-color dinnerware and canisters also reduces visual clutter.

✱ **Update the lighting** to make a new style statement. A chandelier with a rusted-metal finish adds a touch of French country style that's in keeping with the wallpaper design.

✱ **Tone down the brown.** Too much brown wood darkens the room. Cover the table with a light cloth for some visual relief.

Before

Above A busy pattern in a square room creates a feeling of clutter. The dark wainscot gives the eye a place to rest, but it also chops up an already small space.

88

✳ **Unify connecting spaces** and make them feel larger by using a single material for the flooring. Here, new hardwood floors replace the linoleum, tile, and carpet. A large Oriental rug anchors the dining room table and chairs without disrupting the feeling of flow.

Before

makeover **in an hour**

If you have a cupboard in your kitchen or breakfast area, give it a new look each season by changing the display of accessories. Use the examples and tips on these pages to create displays that delight the eye.

Below For the holidays, showcase holiday dishes and mugs, and line the top of the cupboard with collectible decorations.

Below For summer, bring out colorful dishware. Fish, fruit, or flower motifs promote the seasonal theme. Add a houseplant and some fresh flowers to breathe life into the display. A collection of Italian pottery brings warm color to the cupboard top.

Below For fall, echo the warm colors of the pottery with painted glass plates. A plant and tall candlestick replace the framed flower print up top, while the shelf display remains clean and simple, a quiet contrast to the busier look of summer and the holidays.

holidays

summer

fall

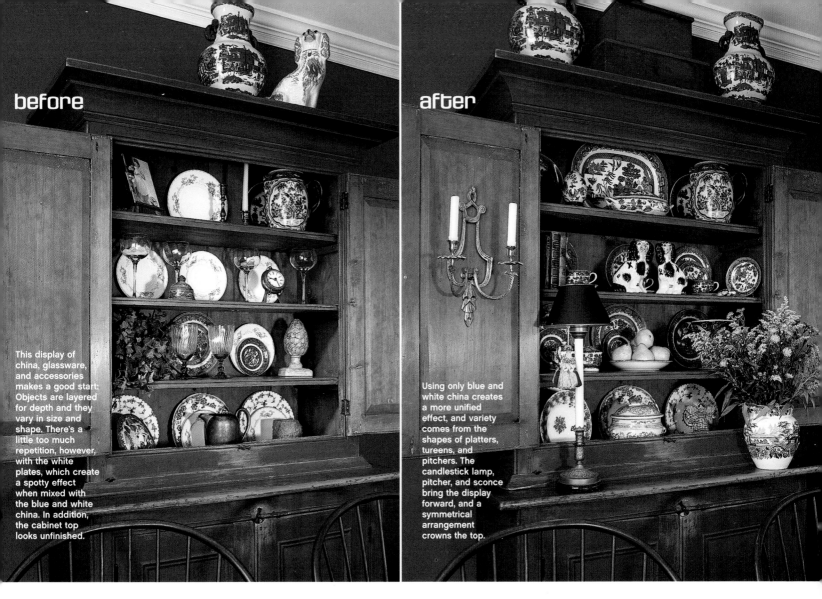

before

This display of china, glassware, and accessories makes a good start: Objects are layered for depth and they vary in size and shape. There's a little too much repetition, however, with the white plates, which create a spotty effect when mixed with the blue and white china. In addition, the cabinet top looks unfinished.

after

Using only blue and white china creates a more unified effect, and variety comes from the shapes of platters, tureens, and pitchers. The candlestick lamp, pitcher, and sconce bring the display forward, and a symmetrical arrangement crowns the top.

✳**Consider function first.** Kitchen cupboards and hutches provide storage as well as display space. Think about organization and storage from an artistic point of view: Instead of piling books haphazardly on various shelves, organize them neatly on the bottom shelf, where they'll be easy to access and where their visual weight will anchor the display. On the shelves above, showcase colorful dinnerware. It's handy when you need to use it and it's a bright focal point when you don't.

✳**Follow the rules of composition** to organize accessories. Repeating a shape—such as a round plate—sets up a rhythm; adding a different shape—such as oval platters or rectangular trays—injects variety and contrast, which keeps the rhythm from becoming boring. Overlap objects, placing smaller ones in front of larger ones, to create depth that pulls the eye into the arrangement. Leave some space between groups of objects to give the eye a place to rest or to emphasize unusual shapes or silhouettes.

✳**Unify with color.** If you vary the heights, sizes, and shapes of the objects, stick to a single color or a family of closely related colors to keep the display from looking chaotic.

✳**Think three-dimensionally** when you decorate the cupboard. Use the lower shelf, which usually projects by several inches, for a small lamp, a pitcher of flowers, or candlesticks. This brings the display into the room.

✳**Go all the way** to the top of the cupboard with accessories. Balance the top arrangement with the bottom display in terms of visual weight. Dark or warm colors appear heavier than light ones.

92

four.personalizewithaccessories

Decorative accessories are like jewelry for your home—the finishing touch that completes the look with a satisfying flourish. In home decorating, accessories include essentials such as lamps, pillows, and area rugs as well as all the objects you collect to hang on walls, arrange on shelves, and display on tabletops. They're usually the last things to be placed when you're redecorating

a room, but that doesn't make them the least significant; accessories add color and texture to rooms, and even more important, they tell your story, reflecting your interests and what you enjoy or cherish.

When you arrange accessories, you're composing a still life. To make it as pleasing as possible, pay attention to repetition, variety, balance, and scale. The principles apply whether you're arranging a collection of vases on a shelf, porcelain boxes on a tabletop, or paintings on a wall. (In fact, the same rules guide how you place furniture in a room.) Working with accessories is fun because you can continually arrange and rearrange, giving yourself new focal points as often as you like.

challenge

To punch up a quiet neutral scheme with accessories that add color and texture. This handsome new home has well-designed, Mission-style architecture and attractive furnishings in the same Mission-inspired style. The spaces need a little "plumping" to take the hard edge off the newness and give the house an established and settled look.

Before

✳ solution

In each room, rearrange, replace, or add accessories to create a comfortably balanced feeling and to enrich the character of the space.

theSPECIFICS

✳ **Make the mantel special.** Choose something unexpected to catch the eye. Stylists Linda Wright and Deborah Hastings moved the print that was hanging over the mantel to the opposite wall and propped a section of wrought-iron fencing on the mantel. Large wooden candlesticks and ceramic vases introduce bolder scale and curvy shapes. They also add touches of color to contrast with the dark leather and wood.

✳ **Dress bare walls.** The space between the windows becomes a secondary focal point when it's occupied by a large print paired with a weightier chest and lamp. Although the chest is a little too tall to serve as an end table, its dark color gives it visual heft that tethers the two armchairs to it.

✳ **Organize bookcases** for more pleasing displays. Rearranging

Before

the books and objects on the shelves creates a clearer rhythm of horizontals, verticals, and negative space (empty areas).

✳ **Use trays or flat-bottomed baskets** to keep stacks of magazines tidy on the coffee table. A woven tray with a waterproof base can also substitute for coasters and protect the surface of the coffee table from spills or messy snacks.

✳ **Lift the eye.** Take accessories all the way to the top of the armoire. The new grouping of objects is simpler but still in scale with the proportions of the furniture. A lot of small items gathered on the top of a large entertainment center will look fussy and unimportant.

✳ **Use plants** to fluff corners and to fill an empty fireplace during the summer. If corners are dimly lit, choose plants that tolerate low light conditions. Lady palms, bamboo palms, and sago palms don't mind low light but may need to be placed on a pedestal to achieve needed height. Ferns need bright to medium light, but for special occasions you can tuck them in front of the fireplace for a lush, exuberant accent.

✳ **Add weight to focal-point pieces** by adding overscale accessories. In the dining room (see page 97), the pie

Top left Pulling the chair and ottoman out of the corner brings them into the conversational grouping. A tall palm softens the corner. The floor lamp stays put since it's important for reading as well as banishing shadows.

Left A chest replaces the wicker-and-wire table between the armchairs. It has greater visual weight to balance the weight of the chairs. Likewise, the urn-shape lamp is heftier and in better scale than the candlestick lamp it replaces.

DINING ROOM

safe seemed lonely, not quite filling the wall space. To bulk up that end of the room, stylists Linda Wright and Deborah Hastings added a large urn filled with bamboo sticks. The light color of the urn partners well with the cupboard, and the sticks supply a strong vertical element without detracting from the pie safe. The original arrangement of orchids, candles, a wire flower, and rattan basket made a pleasing crown for the pie safe. For a change of pace, however, potted ivy and a redware plate can substitute for the basket and candles.

Before

* **Warm up windows** with simple chevron-style valances. The fabric treatment softens the architecture and adds color and pattern without blocking light. Bringing the dark color up high balances the medium brown color of the floor. A plate rack with decorative plates brings dimension and interest to the corner wall.

* **Fill blank spots** with furniture that is both decorative and functional. A handmade painted bench fills the space under the windows and serves as a shelf for plants. (For instructions to make the bench, see page 183.)

* **Dress the table** using a new rag rug spread on the diagonal. This brings touchable texture to

the smooth tabletop. For meals, align the rug with the table edges and use place mats to protect the table from spills.

* **Accent with color.** On the wall above the buffet, a large painting brings vibrant color to the room, replacing a group of four neutral-color prints (not shown). The orange in the artwork picks up the same tones in the buffet and table.

Left If you have a large, heavy framed piece or mirror, consider propping it against the wall instead of hanging it. The furniture becomes a sturdy base for the art.

Opposite Woven-wicker parsons-style chairs look casual and summery. For a different look, try slipcovering them; catalogs offer ready-made slipcovers that fit most chairs of this style.

Before

Before

Left Prints arranged above the plate rail effectively lift the eye upward, but at floor level, the room seems unfinished.

Right The bedroom is clad in the same style paneling as the sunroom, suggesting a similar solution for displaying art.

Below Stair landings are usually overlooked, but wall art above or below the window can make the space more interesting.

SUNROOM

❊ **Add a focus.** The furniture grouping in the sunroom focuses on a blank wall, but the arrangement also puts the seating in the line of sight of anyone in the adjoining kitchen. To provide a focal point, Linda and Deborah brought in a wire plant stand. It fills the empty wall without crowding the small room.

❊ **Seek harmony.** A white wicker chair replaces the brown rattan one, which was moved upstairs. The white wicker better suits the color and mood of the other furnishings and the light walls.

❊ **Combine comfort and function.** An ottoman provides a place for weary feet and doubles as a coffee table. Drinks or food that might damage the fabric can be rounded up on a tray. An upholstered ottoman is more child-friendly than a hard-edged wood coffee table and can be slipcovered with washable fabric if frequent laundering is likely.

Before

STAIR LANDING

❊ **Embellish overlooked spots.** The stair landing doesn't have to be an empty space you barely notice on your way upstairs. A wrought-iron panel that's the same width as the windows fills the area above the chair rail, adding graceful pattern. If your landing is large enough, introduce potted plants for a softening effect.

BEDROOM

❊ **Use the architecture as a guide** in hanging art. The Mission style makes a strong architectural statement in the bedroom, but it presents a challenge for displaying art. To add interest above the wainscot, Linda and Deborah framed black and white photos from the homeowners' vacation and propped them on the molding, along with starfish and seashells, souvenirs from the beach.

❊ **Choose lamps** that are in proportion to the spot they will occupy. Instead of a single tall lamp with a broad shade, a pair of slender candlestick lamps flank the headboard. Their shape complements the vertical emphasis of the paneling.

❊ **Change the look with bedding.** A new comforter in a grid pattern of washed plum and sand works better than the blue and green floral did. It blends better with the wall color and repeats the straight lines of the paneling and furniture.

challenge

To accessorize walls, windows, floor, and furnishings and create an inviting and finished look in a formal dining room.

✳solution

For a fresh take on tradition, use accessories with a contemporary edge to complement 18th-century-style furniture.

theSPECIFICS

✳ Use verticals to link the sideboard to the mirror. A footed bowl and a pair of tall contemporary lamps provide the connection here. To personalize the purchased lampshades, the homeowner glued elegant ribbon fringe around the bottom edges. The circumference of the shades is

Before

Opposite A simple valance hangs by curtain clips from an iron rod. The geometric shape offers a calm contrast to the Baroque curves of the mirror and chairs. A contemporary handcrafted sconce repeats the clean lines of the valance.

Right Sideboards provide storage space as well as a surface for serving when you're entertaining. When the dining room isn't in use, a bowl of flowers or fruit makes the sideboard a focal point.

small enough that she could splurge on a wonderful trim.

 **Anchor with a rug.** A jute rug with a black band gives the room definition; without it, furnishings seem adrift.

 **Use fresh accents.** A bowl of oranges on the table adds a jolt of warm color. You may not be able to keep fresh fruit or flowers in the dining room on a daily basis, but when company comes, these touches add pleasing color and texture and breathe life into a room.

Opposite Add fringe or trim to plain purchased shades. Secure the trim with a heat-resistant silicone glue.

Above left Fill a bowl with fruit, pinecones, marble balls, or glass orbs to dress the table when you're not entertaining.

Left Lighten up a formal dining room by using a contemporary fabric to cover the seats on traditional chairs. The unexpected contrast keeps the room from being staid. A neutral jute rug makes a clean, uncluttered base for the elegant lines of the furnishings.

103

challenge

To tweak the kitchen's decorating personality toward a casual contemporary look. The glass-front cabinets, beaded-board paneling, and wide-plank pine floor could easily suggest country style, but the color scheme of crisp white and ocean blue offers the opportunity to evoke an island mood.

*solution

Display colorful plates and canisters to move the look toward contemporary seashore style. Introduce fabric to help soften hard surfaces and straight lines.

theSPECIFICS

* Use dinnerware decoratively. Four salad plates enliven the wall below the cabinets. Because they're secured with spring-tension plate holders, they're available for use too. Installing the plates below the cupboards keeps the focus low and cozy and makes the room feel more intimate. Alternatively, you could arrange the plates evenly above the cabinets to lift the eye and emphasize an airy sense of space.

* Include a dark accent. The dark blue canisters and a cobalt blue vase give depth to the blue and white color scheme. Any palette will feel more grounded and satisfying if it includes a note that's darker or deeper than the dominant hues.

* Do the balancing act. Visual balance comes into play around the oven, where a fish platter provides the focal point. Decorative and practical items on the left call for equally weighty objects on the right. Interior arrangers Donna

Before

Above The architecture lends itself to country style, but the color scheme could go contemporary or nautical. Accessories can make the difference.

Opposite A scarf and pillow add bright color. You also could cover the chair backs with tie-on slipcovers to soften the lines.

Mobley and Kitty Starling chose an ornamental finial and a bowl of limes for shape and size, but you could also use a crock filled with utensils to serve the same purpose.

✱ **Add softness** with fabrics. A pillow makes the barstool more comfortable and introduces

bold, bright color. Place mats and a scarf draped casually over one stool also help mediate between the white cabinets and blue walls and make the room friendlier and more exciting.

Left Crab shells and seashells accent a pair of paintings that evoke the coastal landscape. Team souvenirs or collectibles with thematically related art to compose a vignette that reminds you of favorite places or events.

challenge

To make a stronger personal style statement in the kitchen and adjoining breakfast room (see page 108–109). When you collect objects that appeal to you, they probably have characteristics in common, such as motif, color, pattern, or decorating style. If they're scattered through the house, however, they may not be expressing your style as clearly as they could.

✳ solution

Bring together items from around the house to uncover a theme that stamps the rooms with new style. Look for interesting shapes and combine them to map an intriguing path for the eye to follow.

theSPECIFICS

✳ **Soften the corner.** Interior arranger Donna Mobley placed a large basket on its side and filled it with good-quality artificial ivy for a lush effect. To keep the basket from rolling out of position, Donna anchored it with another basket that's hidden by the ivy. A colorful vase provides a vertical element and contrasting shape.

✳ **Balance one end** with a grouping at the other end of the cabinets. Donna and fellow arranger Kitty Starling placed two of the wicker chickens in conversation at the refrigerator end of the cabinets. With the addition of woven baskets of different sizes, the chickens equalize the plant and pottery in the opposite corner.

✳ **Link the ends** with a centerpiece. A third grouping of

Before

Above This symmetrical distribution of woven wicker chickens and ivy plants seems a little spotty and sparse.

Opposite Arranging three groups of items that are related in terms of theme or color breaks the long space into attractive rest stops for the eye. Each group is interesting alone, and together they form a pleasing whole.

items continues the farm-animal theme: The folk art tray provides a focal point with a large rectangular shape that gives the eye a place to rest; the porcelain chicken and a rustic mustard-color pot supply contrasting shapes. For a humorous flourish, Donna hung a folk art flying pig from the ceiling. The pig is suspended by monofilament from an eye screw installed in the ceiling with a molly bolt.

BREAKFAST AREA

✳ **Treat the wall as a canvas** or backdrop for a bold display. Three cornice-style plate rails mounted on the wall show off a collection of plates. To add depth and variety to the display, Kitty and Donna positioned smaller items with more vertical shapes along the shelf edges.

✳ **Keep objects in scale** with the space. The new countertop display features items that are large enough to have an impact against the wall area. The items themselves and the rusted finishes suggest French Country style.

✳ **Soften hard edges.** The glass top on the breakfast table seems hard and slick paired with the cane chairs, so Donna and Kitty softened it with a coarse-textured neutral cloth. In keeping with their principle of creating verticals that urge the eye upward, they assembled a centerpiece using topiaries and a garden-statue rabbit.

✳ **Remember the corners.** A tall plant fills the spot where the baker's rack stood. Its sculptural shape adds interest and height but doesn't compete with the focal-point wall.

Above Small items that are spread out evenly and symmetrically along the countertop become lost against the expanse of wall.

Below Wall-mounted plate rails turn the area into a focal point, and large-scale items create a bolder display that takes advantage of the space.

DECORATING STEP-BY-STEP

Assemble a few of your favorite things to create a display that intrigues and pleases the eye every time you look at it. On a mantel, the display becomes an eye-catching focal point, but you can apply the principles shown here to any horizontal surface (tabletop, shelf, cabinet top) that joins a wall.

a few guidelines

* **Use color to unify** a variety of objects. In this example, neutral color and natural textures create underlying harmony.

* **Hang paintings** or mirrors no more than 5 inches above the mantel. If they're higher than that, they'll seem to be floating. Placed lower than that, the piece will look squashed, unless you simply prop it on the mantel. This option works well because the piece is clearly anchored to and supported by the mantel.

* **Arrange items** in groups of three or other odd numbers. This gives the arrangement a casual and natural look. Even numbers can seem stiff.

step 1.

Establish the boundaries for the arrangement by placing one large item at each end of the mantel. Pewter candlesticks with glass hurricane shades do the job here, suggesting a subtle vertical, but you also could use chunkier candlesticks, tall vases, or sconces mounted on the wall. Position these boundary markers above the vertical component of the fireplace (here, the fluted molding) so they won't appear to be falling off the edge of the mantel.

step 2.

Position the largest items first. These will rest against the wall at the back of the mantel shelf. Here, a large square woven basket, chosen to mimic the dark square of the fireplace opening, occupies the left half of the mantel. Next, a print that's about half the height of the basket goes on the other side of an imaginary central line. A small hanging basket with an unusual shape fills the angle between the large basket and the print; the large basket also frames a vintage drawing. When you choose items to feature, select pieces that contrast in shape and size.

step 3.

To fill in around the featured items, experiment with items of different heights, textures, and shapes. Using a lot of glass will fill the space without creating a heavy or overcrowded look. Flowers add life—even something as simple as daisies in cups or juice glasses introduces a fresh feeling. As you position items, allow some to overlap, and leave more space between others. Vary the heights to create peaks and valleys. Overlapping objects, pulling some in front of others, creates depth that draws your eye into the display. Allowing space between objects gives them room to breathe and your eye a place to rest.

111

makeover in an hour

Don't overlook the tops of cabinets and armoires when you're decorating. Taking displays nearly to the ceiling enhances the sense of space. Change the display whenever you need a new view.

It's lonely at the top: Propping a painting on the armoire actually overfills the space below the crown molding. Without additional accessories, the painting looks like it's in storage rather than on display.

An asymmetrical assemblage of old books, candlesticks, tinware, and a sculptural sansevieria plant (also known as mother-in-law's tongue) carves out an interesting up-and-down path for the eye to follow.

before

after

Stylist Linda Wright framed pages from an old calendar and arranged them in three groups on top of the cabinets. Baskets fill in between the groups and balance the display.

✳ **Create peaks and valleys** with an assortment of verticals and horizontals. The vertical objects make the connection between the ceiling and the cabinet, armoire, or shelf. They shouldn't actually brush the ceiling, however, or the display will look cramped and crowded.

✳ **Aim for depth.** If you're working on top of an armoire, arrange the objects along the middle of the top, rather than lining them up along the front or back edges. If you have a painting or basket you want to lean against the wall above the armoire, fill in the space in front of the object with additional accessories that will make a foreground for it. Above cabinets, where the space isn't as deep, create the illusion of depth by positioning smaller, shorter items in front of larger, taller ones.

✳ **Contrast shapes** to keep the eye moving, but provide "bookends" to contain the movement. Candlesticks, boxes, books, or rectangular baskets at each end of the display will keep the round shapes from seeming to roll away.

five.freshen**with**fabric**and**paint

Rearranging furniture and accessories can give your rooms a new attitude and costs nothing more than your time. If you want an even more dramatic change, however, turn to paint and fabric. Paint is the fastest and least expensive way to transform the personality of a room. Before you commit to several gallons of paint, however, browse the local paint store and bring home the color cards

that appeal to you. After you've chosen your favorites, buy a quart of each and apply them to sample pieces of posterboard. Tape these to the wall to see how each color looks under different lighting conditions and with your furnishings. Fabric—whether used for slipcovers, bedding, or window treatments—can redefine your style. If you can sew a straight seam, you can make your own draperies, duvet covers, pillows, and simple slipcovers. Instructions for some of the projects shown on the following pages are included at the back of this book. Also check fabric stores for patterns and instructions for additional styles.

challenge

To wake up a boring entry. Plain white walls drain the fun out of the hip retro style of a 1950s buffet and robotlike metal lamps.

✳solution

Choose a color in the poster and apply it to the wall behind the buffet. An updated version of a popular 1950s color makes the wood tones pop and creates a warm welcome.

thespecifics

✳ **Use color planes** to define the space. Wherever one wall meets another, you can change colors. In this entry, the wall opposite the door receives the dramatic treatment, while the adjacent short wall remains white.

✳ **Make a statement** about your interests with the objects you display. The new wall color enhances the vintage buffet and print as well as the vintage globe (which is a radio) and the McCoy vase.

✳ **Repeat accent colors.** The metal lamps echo the color of the black frame. The robotlike shapes also suit the retro look. The McCoy vase clashes brashly with the chartreuse, recalling popular color combinations in 1950s fabrics and novelty prints.

Before

Above All-white walls in an open-plan house are safe but boring.

Opposite To use different wall colors in an open-plan house, follow this general rule: Wherever one plane or flat area meets another, start a new color. If you enjoy lots of color, use contrasting hues. For a quieter effect, choose colors that are closely related.

117

challenge

To create a more dramatic and sophisticated look in the dining room. The wall color doesn't enhance the color of the wood furnishings, but the homeowner doesn't want to change it. The large return-air grille (see page 120) is in the direct line of sight from the front door and because the grille was painted to match the white trim, it attracts attention it doesn't deserve.

* solution

Introduce a new color scheme with a rug, draperies, and accessories. Slipcover the chair seats to downplay the forest of legs and paint the return-air grille to match the wall.

thespecifics

* **Choose a patterned rug** that contains a note of the wall color but takes the color scheme in a different direction. A rug in a range of dark greens grounds the table and chairs and defines a cohesive look for the room.

* **Add color with fabric.** Using the green in the rug as a guide, stylist Deborah Hastings replaced the gauzy, lightweight draperies with green velvet panels and added light green fabric to the inside back of the china cabinet. In the cabinet, the

Above Too much brown wood and too many legs make the dining room look uninviting.

Opposite Sheer chair skirts add blocks of solid color to give some relief to the eye. A dark rug and draperies supply warmth and sophistication.

Right Green fabric wrapped around foam-core board fits snugly against the back of the china cabinet and shows off the china.

fabric enhances the creamy white of the china better than the dark wood did. (For instructions on adding a fabric backing, see page 176.)

✳ **Emphasize the windows** by mounting the drapery rod higher than the top of the window. To fill the space above the window, add an architectural ornament, such as a piece of wrought-iron or architectural salvage.

✳ **Reinforce the color scheme** with art and accessories. Framed postcards featuring bird prints make inexpensive artwork for the window wall. Dried flower arrangements in wall baskets replace artwork on each side of the china cabinet.

The colors pick up the hues of the rug, and the formal Biedermeier style of the arrangements, with flowers placed in rows of color, suits the new sophistication. The arrangements are hung high enough to clear the two armchairs, which stand against the wall when they're not in use.

✳ **Paint out distracting details.** Save attention-getting color contrasts for architectural features you want to highlight. The return-air grille can't be covered up, but painting it to match the walls makes it disappear.

✳ **Create a secondary focal point.** Positioning a narrow wrought-iron table in front of the grille draws attention away from the fixture and creates an attractive focus for visitors, who see the wall when they enter the house. (For instructions on making a similar marble-top table, see page 179). With the marble-tile

surface, the table can also serve as a buffet for hot dishes. Botanical prints from a calendar, matted with light green, reinforce the new color scheme. Tall lamps provide the necessary link between the tabletop and wall art and also warm the room with mood-setting light at night.

✳ **Downplay chair and table legs** and tone down some of the brown wood with chair skirts. These tie over the seat cushions without hiding them entirely. Using a sheer fabric yields a soft, summery effect, and the white color echoes the white woodwork and

the white china (see page 177 for instructions on making the slipcovers). For a winter look, you could make skirts from a dark green velvet to match the draperies. A scarf made from paisley fabric softens the table without completely covering the wood. (To make one, cut a 52-inch square and stitch $\frac{1}{2}$ inch from the outside edges. Then pull out threads from the raw edges to create a fringe.) The scarf dresses the table when the table is not in use and it can be left in place when entertaining.

Before

Above The dining room wall with the return-air grille is immediately visible from the front door. Painting it to match the white trim calls unwanted attention to it.

Right Chair skirts downplay the abundance of legs and brown wood. For special occasions, make little bouquets of dried flowers and tie them to the chair backs with ribbon.

Opposite A wrought-iron table supports a new top, made from marble tiles from a home center. It draws attention away from the return-air grille without blocking it.

challenge

To bring warmth and casual comfort to a combination sitting room and kitchen dominated by stark white walls and formal traditional furniture.

✳ solution

Add color to the walls and relax the formality of the camelback sofa with a slipcover.

theSPECIFICS

Above Instead of enhancing the traditional furnishings, the all-white walls absorb the shapes into the background. The lampshades virtually disappear.

Below Using architectural salvage and old door knobs as accessories introduces a comfortable weathered warmth.

✳ **Look to accessories** for color cues. A collection of decorative plates inspired the medium blue chosen for the walls. The color enhances the rosy red upholstery of the chairs as well as the warm, dark wood tones. Keeping the trim and cabinetry white makes the blue look crisp, not chilly.

✳ **Slipcover for casual ease.** The eye reads the red-and-white pinstripe fabric on the sofa as rosy pink, so the slipcover balances the stronger red of the two upholstered chairs. (Solid red would have been too heavy visually.) The slipcover also disguises the formal shape of the sofa.

✳ **Rearrange furniture** for better balance. Moving the sofa so that its back is to the kitchen creates a cozier feeling in the sitting area. Bringing a wicker table in from outdoors and using salvaged architectural pieces as accessories further relaxes the area with weathered textures.

challenge

To add architectural charm and pizzazz to a bland, all-white kitchen.

✳ solution

Give flat-front cabinets classic character by applying screen molding to simulate paneling. Accent cabinetry with new hardware. Perk up walls with paint and a wallpaper border.

thespecifics

* **Cut screen molding** (available at home improvement centers and lumberyards) to fit the dimensions of each door. Plan for the vertical side pieces to run from the top to the bottom edge of each door; fit the horizontal top and bottom strips inside these with butt joints. The vertical center piece fits inside the frame, and the horizontal crossbars fit snugly between the vertical strips. Check that corners are square. Glue the moldings to the doors and tack with brads. Prime the entire door and paint to match the cupboard facings. (Look for a primer that's recommended for use on both raw wood and glossy painted surfaces.) Use a similar procedure to give the drawers a facelift.

* **Install new hardware.** Cobalt blue pulls and flower-shape handles add dollops of bold color, accenting the lively scheme of yellow, yellow-green, and blue. If the new drawer hardware doesn't match the old holes, fill the holes and sand them before painting the drawer and drilling new ones.

* **Paint the walls.** A green that resembles the color of Granny Smith apples energizes the space. The wallpaper border supplies the cue for the yellow and blue accents and accessories.

* **Keep windows simple** with white wood-slat blinds. These provide light control and privacy, and the strong horizontal lines echo the paneled effect on the cabinet doors and drawers.

Before

Opposite Screen molding transforms flat, contemporary cabinet doors and drawers into more traditional-looking paneled ones.

125

challenge

To update a dark, old-fashioned kitchen without remodeling.

✳solution

Paint the cabinets and walls to freshen the space, and remove cabinet doors to brand the room with new country style.

theSPECIFICS

✳ **Use what you have.** Mock tongue-and-groove paneling on the cabinet doors and drawer fronts serves as a template for painting these surfaces in wide stripes. The low-contrast combination of pale periwinkle and white makes the room feel airier and lighter. To paint kitchen cabinets and drawers, remove the doors and drawers. Apply a primer formulated for glossy or wood veneer surfaces. This eliminates the need for tedious sanding and helps the paint adhere well. Paint the cabinets, doors, and drawers with a hard-wearing latex enamel suitable for kitchens and baths. Paint the walls with scrubbable semi-gloss or low-sheen latex.

✳ **Replace the old knobs** with bin-style pulls to enhance the new country style. If you can't find these at your local hardware store or home improvement center, check home furnishings catalogs.

✳ **Remove upper cabinet doors** to show off dinnerware. This does require a certain degree of tidiness, but it also lets you enjoy the colors and shapes of your favorite dishes and glassware. Open shelves also make the room feel more expansive.

✳ **Dress windows** with half shutters for privacy. A hanging shelf takes advantage of light to grow herbs.

Before

Above Brown tongue-and-groove cabinetry looks dark and dated. Fortunately, paint offers a relatively easy and inexpensive solution.

challenge

To redo a guest room, keeping the bold red walls as the starting point. The white beds, bedding, lamp, and table contrast sharply with the walls, and the room awaits the softening effects of art and accessories.

Before

✳solution

Use the bed skirts to develop a more complex color scheme with bedding, draperies, and accessories.

thespecifics

✳ **Start with bedding.** Duvets and neck roll pillows made from plaid and a coordinating toile bring the wall color to the beds. The prints also tone down the dazzling effect of snowy white matelassé coverlets and white-painted woodwork. Pillow shams stitched from an oversize green and white check provide a color break between the headboard and the matelassé sham. (For bed skirt, duvet, and neck roll instructions, see pages 179–181.)

✳ **Be inventive with wall art.** The decorative plates hanging over each bed look like a collection of English transferware, but they're actually high-quality 8-inch-diameter paper plates. (Look for something similar at party goods stores.)

✳ **Freshen the lampshade** by painting it with wide olive green stripes. To make the stripes, apply 1$\frac{1}{2}$-inch-wide painter's tape to the shade, spacing the tape about $\frac{1}{4}$ inch apart at the

top edge and about 5 inches apart at the bottom edge (measurements will vary, depending on the size of the shade). Use a pencil to lightly draw along the edges of the tape; then pull the tape away and paint inside the pencil lines. You may need to apply two or three coats if the shade material is absorbent.

✳ **Soften the windows** with simple draperies and an unstructured valance. Both are made with rod pockets and gathered onto metal curtain rods. For a custom-finished look, stylist Linda Wright edged the draperies with the same scalloped trim she used on the neck roll pillows. A coordinating bobble fringe embellishes the hem of the valance. Linda used the same fringe to dress up gingham pillows made by an upholsterer. She had them constructed with a zipper closure so she could add the fringe herself, using a double-sided adhesive tape to hold the fringe in place while she stitched.

✳ **Restyle an old chest of drawers** with a fresh coat of paint, new wooden knobs, and new feet. Linda used fence post finials from a home improvement center to make the feet. She painted the finials white and attached each one to a block of wood, using a double-end screw; then she screwed each block of wood into a corner of the underside of the chest.

Before

Left Paint and new knobs change the look of a simple dresser, but stylist Linda Wright took the project a step further by adding turned feet. The secret? Fence post finials from a home improvement center, attached to blocks of wood with double-end screws.

Opposite: An old love seat reupholstered in plaid fabric adds comfort to the guest room. Flanked by matching mail-order tables, the small love seat turns the bump-out into a window seat.

Below: Keep accessories simple in the guest room so visitors will have space for their own toiletries or necessities.

challenge

To turn a bedroom and bath into a multipurpose retreat. Painting the walls yellow is the first step in turning the room into a sunny, serene place for sleeping and working. The next steps must take into account the iron bed and wicker bedside table, which need to stay.

*solution

Import fresh, happy color with fabrics, accessories, and custom shutters that pop into the window frame.

theSPECIFICS

* **Angle the bed** across the corner to give access from both sides. This also makes the room look more welcoming. Pull the wicker table close to the bed and replace the candlestick lamp with a new lamp better designed for reading. (The new lamp can take a higher-wattage bulb, and the angle of the shade throws light in a wider circle.)

* **Go merrily monochromatic** with the color scheme to enlarge the sense of space and maximize the impact of your favorite color. On the bed, a yellow coverlet and buttercream sheets over a textured white bed skirt blend with the walls.

* **Avoid tiny rugs.** A blue and white throw rug seemed lost on the bare wood floor. A room-size jute rug is in better proportion to the room, and its natural oatmeal color lightens the dark wood.

* **Look for double-duty pieces.** Instead of stacked wicker chests at the foot of the bed, designers Gary McKay and

Before

Above It's hard to make the bed when it's pushed into the corner. Although yellow, blue, and white can compose a successful color scheme, there's not enough repetition here to make it work.

132

Tricia Foley brought in a bench. Besides offering a place to sit, it serves as a catchall for books and clothes. To maintain the color scheme, the designers chose a bench with a yellow frame and white webbing.

✳ Explore window options. If you need privacy but don't care for curtains, consider investing in shutters made to fit the windows (see page 192 for sources). Custom-order pre-hung shutters come in frames tailored to fit your windows and easily pop into place. Painted white to match the woodwork, they blend seamlessly with the architecture. In the bathroom, pre-hung shutters mask the too contemporary glass-block window, creating a softer country look (see page 136).

✳ Opt for movable storage pieces. If you lack big closets but have the wall space, bring in a cupboard or armoire for extra storage. Shop garage sales or flea markets, where you might find a piece that only needs cleaning up and painting. If you need to replace wobbly or warped shelves, have plywood or pine shelving cut to fit at a lumberyard and use the old shelf supports as a guide for installing new ones. Use boxes and baskets to keep things tidy and organized inside the cupboard. Hampers on top provide storage space for linens or out-of-season clothing. Old picnic baskets work well here, too; the lids protect the contents from dust. Lidded straw baskets that can slide under the bed provide more storage for out-of-season items.

✳ Tuck in comfy seating. Angling the bed can open up a spot for a chair in one corner. An upholstered rocking chair slipcovered in yellow cotton maintains the buttery color scheme in this room and provides good back support for reading or working.

✳ Add color and softness with fabric. In the bathroom (see page 136), a bold mustard and white check fabric encloses the bathtub and skirts the sink. The fabric softens the room and hides unsightly plumbing.

✳ Cover up the flooring. If the bathroom flooring is a color or material you don't care for, lay a jute runner over it to lighten the space. The hard-wearing jute won't be damaged by water.

Below Custom-order pre-hung shutters pop into the window frames to provide privacy and light control and a clean, architectural look. For a fabric alternative, install shades or roller blinds. Check fabric stores for roller-blind kits you can cover with fabric.

Below To enhance the impression of elbow-room, keep walls, furnishings, and fabrics in the same family of hues. Painting the chest of drawers a creamy white echoes the color of the woodwork and the bed; the chest seems to disappear into the yellow walls.

Below Lidded woven baskets make excellent underbed storage, but they're also pretty enough to display. A natural jute floor covering bounces light up into the room to expand the sense of space.

Above Organize magazines in file boxes made for the purpose (look for them at office-supply stores). Matching lidded boxes hold photos, stationery, or work supplies and keep shelves tidy. Choose boxes to match your color scheme to maintain a unified look.

Left Instead of using regular bookshelves, consider recycling an old armoire or cupboard. In a multipurpose room, the shelves can hold work supplies or clothing—or both. If you have room to keep the door open, decorate it as if it were wall space.

Right Glass-block windows strike a discordantly contemporary note in the bathroom. The tile floor is handsome but dark, and the exposed plumbing isn't particularly attractive.

Opposite Custom-order pre-hung shutters mounted over the window opening mask the glass block with a more traditional look. A larger rug minimizes the dark tile.

Below left An étagère supplies needed storage space for towels and toiletries.

Below right A single-pleat skirt attaches to the edge of the countertop with hook-and-loop tape to hide the plumbing.

Before

✳ **Restyle the bathroom mirror.** The original was a plain sheet of glass; to dress it up and blend it with the 1920s architecture, the designers assembled a frame from molding, painted it white, and installed it over the mirror.

✳ **Add mood lighting.** The candlestick lamp from the bedroom comes into the bathroom to provide soft light. If you have room in your bathroom for a small decorative lamp, it's a comforting addition. A low-watt bulb banishes darkness, sheds a friendly glow, and helps guests find their way at night.

challenge

To give style and personality to a guest room that lacks character.

✳solution

Warm the walls with a soft, pale neutral that shows off the dark pencil-post beds. Use accessories that relate to the home's location (here, a coastal area) to bring the outdoors inside without being too "themed."

theSPECIFICS

✳ **Employ contrast** for character. A soft beige paint on the walls adds warmth yet still allows the beds to take center stage. Interior designer Sandy Lucas uses this kind of high contrast between walls and furnishings to create interest in a room when the architecture is bland. A black finish on the beds, the picture frames, bedside chest, lampshade, and rug create unity. New bedding plays on the theme in a lighter key.

✳ **Provide amenities.** The old bedside table was too low to be useful. Because the beds are high and the space between them limited, Sandy had a chest custom-made to fit the spot. The stained-wood top keeps it from looking too heavy.

Before

Right and Opposite A fishing-creel lamp and antique prints of coastal scenes bring the home's setting inside.

138

Stacked suitcases and a wicker
fishing creel mask some of the
legginess of one bed, connecting
it visually to the floor.

challenge

To impart interest and character to a basic beach house bedroom. The white modular furniture was a given, chosen for durability and accommodating a crowd of boys.

✳solution

To make up for the absence of interesting architectural details, use contrasting color on beds and walls to supply the flair the room needs.

theSPECIFICS

✳ **Select a color scheme.** Using the nautical flags for inspiration, Sandy Lucas chose a primary scheme of bold red, yellow, and blue. The red goes on the walls because it's vibrant, warm, and comforting.

✳ **Balance the walls** with bedding. Blue sheets and white bed frames suggested the patriotic motif of a flag-inspired area rug. Pillows add color accents and comfort.

Before

Above Plain white walls and white furniture make for a stark and sterile setting.

Right The mattresses are fitted with color-coordinated sheets, but because making up bunk beds is awkward, the boys pull out sleeping bags and lay them on top.

Opposite The poster over the chest of drawers features the nautical flag alphabet. Designer Sandy Lucas used the flags as inspiration for the color scheme and for the custom-designed accent pillows, which can be arranged to spell the homeowners' last name.

challenge

To refresh a dowdy bedroom and turn it into a sophisticated master-suite retreat. The colonial-style furniture looks like a set piece with everything perfectly matched. (The bedside lamps are mismatched but neither one is in scale with the bed or the bedside tables.) The high contrast between the dark bedspread, furnishings, and valance (see page 144) and the light wall color seems disjointed rather than dramatic and doesn't create a restful atmosphere.

Before

Above One lamp is too large and the other too small, and the dark furniture and bedspread don't relate well to the wall color.

✱ solution

Choose a new wall color and new bedding for a monochromatic scheme, replace the bedside tables with unmatched ones, and dress the windows with new draperies. A new reclining chair and window seat complete the transformation.

THESPECIFICS

✱ **Paint the walls.** A warm taupe wraps the room in serene, understated color. New bedding and window treatments are in the same warm neutral range for a quiet, elegant effect.

Left Covered buttons, fringe, and welting give pillows a custom-finished look, but if you can sew a straight line, you can make these yourself. Look for pillow patterns at fabric stores for guidelines on yardage requirements and assembly techniques.

The combination of coverlet and a tailored bed skirt produces a more sophisticated look than a spread that drapes to the floor.

Left A tailored pleated skirt covers an ordinary decorator table to stand at one side of the bed. The glass top protects the fabric and provides a stable surface.

Right Floor-length draperies topped by a valance create a strong vertical line that makes the standard 8-foot ceiling seem higher.

Below left Under the window seat skirt and cushion is a box built from 2x4s and plywood. It provides storage and seating in the dormer.

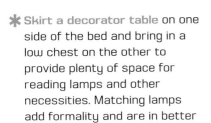

Before

✱ **Skirt a decorator table** on one side of the bed and bring in a low chest on the other to provide plenty of space for reading lamps and other necessities. Matching lamps add formality and are in better scale with the bed; unmatched lamps could work here too, if their bases were of equal visual weight and the bottom edges of the lampshades were aligned.

✱ **Replace the mirror.** Stylist Linda Wright removed the

A decorative mirror over the dresser suggests a more "evolved" or collected look—objects and furnishings acquired over time—than the three-part mirror that came with the dresser.

three-part mirror that came with the dresser (not shown) and in its place, she centered a single mirror in a decorative frame. The two-toned wooden frame harmonizes with the dark color of the dresser but contrasts with the style for an interesting, eclectic effect.

✳ **Create a reading spot.** A new, comfortable recliner and floor lamp fill the corner formerly occupied by the television. (The TV now sits on the dresser.)

✳ **Put odd spaces to use.** In the dormer, Linda built a window seat with a top that lifts for storage and covered it with a skirt (see pages 181–183 for instructions on making the window seat and skirt).

challenge

To use the psychological effect of color to make the living and dining areas seem cooler in the summer and warmer in the winter, using fabrics and accessories that satisfy the contrasting color preferences of the homeowners.

✱ solution

Start with an Oriental rug as the palette for a rich, cozy winter decorating scheme; then switch to white cotton slipcovers for summer. Change accessories with the seasons to reinforce the impact of color on the perceived temperature.

thespecifics

✱ **Go warm for winter.** With an Oriental rug as the starting point, interior designer Catheryn Wilson chose a blue cotton damask for the sofa and a floral tapestry for a pair of French chairs and an ottoman. The patterns in the tapestry and the rug are different in scale but share the same colors so they're compatible partners. A blue and cream stripe for the antique settee

Left Brass candlesticks, a wooden tray, and touches of red bring warm winter color to the coffee table.

Opposite Busy patterns on the floor and armchairs heat up the energy level in the room. A striped fabric on the 19th-century French settee balances the florals.

146

148

repeats the color of the sofa and provides a geometric foil for the florals.

✱ **Continue the thread of color** into adjoining spaces. Wine red fabric covers the barstool seats and backs, and a deep blue is used to upholster the breakfast room chairs (see page 150). For winter, three layers of tablecloths convey a rich warmth, and the kitchen shelves display red toleware and ceramics. Antique old-master-style paintings of fruits take the berry colors to the walls, and heavy gilt frames gleam with warm highlights.

✱ **Use the mantel for impact.** Wine-red tole planters frame an antique painting of a palace interior. The dominant red hues of the painting bring the reds of the barstools and breakfast room back into the living room.

Opposite Red upholstery on the barstools and French still lifes on the wall carry winter warmth to the kitchen and breakfast area.

Right and above right A painting of a palace interior by early-20th-century artist Malva Shalek emanates warm color above the mantel shelf. Red tole planters frame the painting to underscore the toasty effect.

Layering the breakfast table with three cloths supplies a large block of color in this room and suggests rich warmth.

Leaving the table bare and covering the chairs with tailored white skirts breathes a fresh, airy feeling into the room. Blue and white china on the kitchen shelves and botanical prints on the walls emphasize the summery theme.

✱ **Go white for summer.** Because one of the homeowners prefers off-white upholstery, Catheryn suggested slipcovering everything, even the barstools, in creamy white for summer. "They loved the idea of completely changing the look with the seasons," she says. A crewel-patterned natural cotton covers the French chairs and ottoman and a tone-on-tone striped cotton blend dresses the sofa. A basket-weave washed cotton covers the barstools and breakfast room chair seats (for instructions on making barstool slipcovers, see page 188).

✱ **Change accessories** on the mantel, coffee table, and walls to reflect the lighter look. On the mantel, stone urns filled with magnolia leaves replace the tole planters. On the coffee table, a white tray and footed bowl replace red books and a gold-tone tray. Botanical prints supplant the paintings in both rooms. In the breakfast area, a white planter serves as a centerpiece, and on the kitchen shelves, a china collection brings the colors of sea and sky indoors.

✱ **Lighten up with bare wood.** In summer, bare wood floors in the breakfast area look cool and clean.

Opposite Roll up the rug for a cool-to-the-toes look. White fabrics in a variety of textures look clean, uncluttered, and welcoming.

Top right On the mantel, white stone and a cream-colored garden ornament bring a summery theme into the room.

Right White slipcovers transform the barstools for the season too.

makeover in an hour

tabletops and dressers are staging areas for secondary focal points. give yourself new views by creating pleasing compositions, using favorite collections or materials that reflect the seasons.

There's not enough variety in size and shape of objects here. Although the tallest pitcher connects the dresser to the painting, the lineup of items doesn't create an interesting path.

This display delights the eye with objects placed at different levels to trace an interesting path across the dresser. Items with different sizes and shapes also create depth leading back to the painting.

154

before

after

✳ **Decorate with silver** or pewter for an old-world elegance. A loose line of candles and containers along the center of the table serves as a centerpiece for a dinner party and will make the table an attractive focal point even when you're not entertaining. Stagger the items in the line so it looks casual, not rigid. Pewter or silver candlesticks and pitchers filled with roses work for summer or winter.

✳ **Evoke Tuscan gardens** with evergreen topiaries in terra-cotta pots. Pile a terra-cotta planter with pears to tie the topiaries together. (To save on the number of pears you'll need, fill the planter with crumpled newspaper to within an inch or so of the rim; then arrange the pears on top.) To protect the table surface from moisture damage, rest the topiary pots on coasters. To prevent infestations of spider mites, which can be a problem in dry indoor environments, give the plants a gentle shower of lukewarm water every couple of weeks.

BALANCING ACT

WHAT'S WRONG WITH THIS PICTURE?

RIGHT HEIGHT

Finding the right end table to partner with a chair or sofa is a little like Goldilocks's dilemma: One is too tall; another is too short. How to find the one that's just right? Let the height of your sofa or chair arm guide you. The tabletop should be no more than 3 inches taller or shorter than the arm of the seating piece. It should be easy to reach so you don't have to stretch up, down, or out and around to pick up a cup of tea or lay down a book. The table should also suit the style of the seating piece. And if a reading lamp is on the table, the lamp needs to be tall enough for the light to fall over your shoulder. The wood pedestal in the top photo is too tall for the sofa arm and it's too hefty; the sofa looks out of scale. The table in the bottom photo is too short; the lamp throws light too low to be helpful, and a person sitting on the sofa would have to stretch out and around the sofa arm to reach items on the table.

DO

Left Two rustic wood boxes stack to the right height for this sofa, and the vintage look suits the casual sofa style. A floor lamp with an adjustable neck can be turned to the desired angle for reading.

Below Although you have some leeway, the perfect height for an end table is an inch or two shorter than the arm of the chair or sofa.

DO

Above For reading, the bottom of the lampshade should be slightly above shoulder height when you're seated on the sofa.

Left The pedestal height is perfect for a sofa with high arms, and the reading light can be aimed where you need it. It's not the ideal spot for a cup of tea, however, because you'd have to reach up and over the arm.

six.buildinginstyle

If you're handy with a saw (or you know someone who is), you can add style, function, and character to rooms with simple woodworking projects. Even if you have to hire out the work, makeovers that tiptoe into the realm of remodeling can so dramatically alter the way a room looks and functions that the investment will amply reward you. You'll enjoy your home more and you'll have increased its value.

Adding crown molding to a room or painting and rehanging kitchen cabinets may be jobs you'd prefer to leave to professionals, but any experienced do-it-yourselfer can add molding to plain cabinet doors, build a louvered cornice for .a shower, or attach sections of architectural salvage to a door frame. Along with the more involved projects in this chapter, you'll find ideas for little touches (no experience required) that can have a big impact—such as replacing ordinary drawer pulls with artist-made handles to give a bathroom or kitchen a brand-new look, or using unexpected items to whip up your own artwork. The result? More personality for your rooms.

challenge

To transform a guest suite from a makeshift collection of castoffs into a comfortable and inviting bedroom and bath. These two rooms had never been decorated beyond the owner's initial painting of the walls in blue and white stripes. The bedroom is furnished with leftovers from the rest of the house, and the daybed is rigged from two headboards, which are too tall. A skirted table, squeezed into the corner, blocks access to the window and makes the room feel cramped. The bathroom has an ordinary vanity and countertop and a wall-mounted plate glass mirror.

Above Too much furniture and headboards that are too tall create a crowded feeling in the guest bedroom. In addition, too many patterns compete for attention.

✳ solution

Build a new frame for the daybed, using 2x6 boards and dowels. Replace bedding and pillows to clarify the color scheme and supply comfort. In the bathroom, paint the walls, install a louvred enclosure for the shower, and craft a frame for the mirror to give the space a fun, breezy spirit.

theSPECIFICS

✳ **Build a new bed frame.** Give a daybed a whole new look with arms inspired by Chippendale-style garden benches. Homeowner and stylist Deborah Hastings designed and built the roll-arm frame herself, using standard lumber and a table saw (see page 187 for step-by-step instructions). The daybed frame is mounted high enough on the arms to allow a trundle bed to be tucked underneath.

✳ **Downplay distracting pattern.** For a cleaner, more sophisticated look, Deborah replaced the gathered dust ruffle and wedding-ring quilt with a tailored skirt and solid white matelassé coverlet. To bring the colors of the painting

Before

into the room, she selected a medley of pillows keyed to the artwork. Her trick for choosing the right colors? She collected paint chips that matched the colors in the painting and the stripes on the wall and glued them to an index card that she carried with her when she went shopping.

* **Relieve crowding** by removing furniture that's too big. With the skirted table gone, Deborah can reach the window to open it. A small tray table provides a place for necessities, and it's easy to move when the trundle bed needs to be pulled out. Floor lamps, to be added later, will provide reading light.

* **Lighten with paint.** In the bathroom, Deborah covered the dark green-gold walls with a lighter yellow-gold. After the paint dried, she applied a white top coat and dragged a comb through the wet paint. "It was impossible to be neat and perfect with the wave, so I

deliberately kept it freehand and unstructured," she says.

* **Restyle cabinetry.** To add interest to the plain vanity doors, Deborah cut and painted screening lath to fit inside the molding in an X shape (see page 186 for instructions). She also replaced the brass knobs with new glass ones.

* **Frame the mirror.** Using glass tiles and seashells, Deborah turned this boring mirror into a focal point with personality. (For instructions, see page 185.)

* **Add architecture.** A louvred cornice made from lumber, lath, and MDF board hides the shower rod (for instructions, see page 184). The curtains at each side are fixed in place so the effect is that of a window with draperies; a clear liner with a lace topper keeps shower water from splashing into the room.

* **Make your own "art."** Deborah mounted flip-flops on matboard and hung them on the wall to suggest a vacation theme.

Before

Above "What was I thinking with this paint?" exclaims Deborah. Covering it with a yellow-gold base followed by a white top coat was the first step in transforming the room.

Top left Standard cabinets and an unframed mirror result in a cookie-cutter look.

Top center The new combed paint treatment—deliberately free-form—adds liveliness to the walls.

Top right A louvered panel dresses up the shower without trapping steam.

challenge

To refurbish the kitchen in an 1895 Victorian home, working within a limited budget and preserving the architectural integrity of the house.

✳ solution

Paint the cabinets instead of replacing them. Replace laminated plastic countertops with a simple, classic white tile and remove the laminated plastic cladding on the wall behind the oven to reveal original brick. Paint walls and add a couple of statement-piece antiques; these give the room the comfortable look of an English-style unfitted kitchen, with movable furniture supplementing built-in cabinets.

the SPECIFICS

✳ **Put function first.** Homeowners Patricia and Paul Hansen replaced the sink unit with a corner sink and cabinet to make better use of space. The old arrangement crowded the dishwasher and created a dead corner that was too hard to reach to be useful.

✳ **Add architectural character** with crown molding. Capping the walls and cabinets with traditional-style molding restores the architectural detailing that's in keeping with the woodwork around the windows and doors. The homeowners also raised the

Before

Above The cabinets were in good condition, but the sink crowded the dishwasher and created an awkward, hard-to-use corner.

Opposite The corner sink makes more efficient use of space. White ceramic tile replaces the laminated plastic countertops and covers the backsplash.

upper cabinets to create more space underneath for open shelves suspended from spindles. Patricia displays mugs and glassware here.

✳ **Warm up with color.** With white tile countertops and off-white woodwork, Patricia didn't want all-white cabinets and walls. For the cabinets, she chose a soft, subtle gray-green. After much experimentation with shades of terra-cotta for the walls, she spotted a warm gray and immediately knew it was the right hue (see page 192 for details). It proved to be even more successful than she had anticipated—suddenly the red tile floor, which had been an eyesore, looked perfect. The paint color also makes a dramatic backdrop for the couple's collection of antique black and white Wedgwood

transferware.

✳ **Be bold with hardware.** Hand-painted porcelain knobs from Mackenzie Childs add an artistic flourish to the drawers. Such knobs can be pricey, but when there are only five or six in the room, they're an affordable luxury and have a decorative impact far greater than their cost. (Such items are so distinctive that they are more effective in limited numbers.)

✳ **Opt for the furnished look.** Repurposing antique furniture for kitchen duty takes the hard edges off the space. "I needed an island and found an old library table for $700," says Patricia. For another $700, she had a marble top cut and attached to the table. To raise the table to a more comfortable height for working, Patricia added bun feet from a home

Right High ceilings and low cabinets meant wasted space.

Opposite Raising the upper cabinets made room for new dropped shelves underneath. An old library table, fitted with a new marble top, serves as a spacious work island.

Before

improvement store. For storage, she found an antique cupboard that fits perfectly between the windows. An antique chair gives company a place to perch.

Clockwise from top Handpainted porcelain knobs for doors and drawers pack a lot of decorative punch. (Check home improvement centers, kitchen design shops, and catalogs for knobs made from metal, resin, porcelain, or glass in a variety of designs and motifs.) The new sink configuration opens up counter space for a potted herb garden. When laminated plastic behind the oven was removed, the original brick wall was revealed. Warm gray walls show off the antique Wedgwood transferware.

Opposite An antique cupboard fits perfectly between the windows to provide additional kitchen storage.

challenge

To give vintage architectural character to a dated 1960s addition. This two-level sitting area was once a screened porch that was later enclosed and remodeled with sliding glass doors, dark-stained beams, and dark hardwood floors. The lower level, which is off the kitchen, serves as a pass-through area to the sliding glass doors, so it can't be used effectively for either seating or storage. An adjacent room is a nonfunctional space with no natural light.

✳ solution

Lighten the space and change its appearance from utilitarian to inviting by installing new windows, refinishing floors, and whitewashing beams. Use architectural salvage for vintage charm.

theSPECIFICS

✳ Replace the windows. The sliding glass doors that had been installed in both levels of the sitting area were replaced with single-pane windows. To give the windows a more traditional look, homeowner Donna Bokland added ready-made mullions from a home improvement center. She purchased them unfinished and painted them white, then cut them to fit the window frames.

Left Steps lead from a pass-through area to a sitting area where sliding glass doors overlooked a pool and deck.

Right The pass-through area is now a window seat off the kitchen. Single-pane windows acquire traditional style, thanks to pop-in mullions.

* **Refinish the floors.** The original hardwood flooring on the stairs and upper level was stripped of its dark stain and left natural. Donna had it coated with a waterbase polyurethane for protection.

* **Lighten the dark beams.** Donna applied four coats of whitewash, using a soft 4-inch-wide paintbrush. The first two coats were about 70 percent water and 30 percent paint; the final two coats were half water, half paint.

* **Convert wasted space.** An L-shape bench built into the lower level now provides both seating and storage. The bench top lifts for easy access. The coffee table is an old pine farm table that Donna cut down to the desired height.

* **Use architectural salvage** to add character. A newel post cut in half rounds off the rough beam that frames the opening between the sitting area and the studio. The other half was attached to the wall to serve as a handrail along the short

Before

Above White walls and floors stripped of stain bring an airy cottage feeling to the sitting room.

Left Donna Bokland collects architectural salvage and uses it to create birdhouses and sculpture. She also applied salvaged materials to the door frames, walls, and stairwell of her home.

stairway from the lower level to the seating area.

✳ **Take advantage of "accidents."** When the grass-cloth wallcovering was pulled off, it left the wall "a mess," Donna says. But it was in perfect condition for receiving an aged-looking fresco treatment. The wall was washed to remove all traces of wallpaper adhesive; then it was primed and painted a "dirty neutral." Artist Anita Medina then used layered glazes to paint scenes in the style of ancient Roman frescoes along the stairwell wall.

Wrap Ties and
Tie at Back

seven.projects

Do-it-yourself projects let you put your personal stamp on furnishings and accessories so your rooms reflect your individual sense of style. Even beginning sewers can make pillow covers, duvets, and more. The slipcovers illustrated on the following pages may be a little more challenging, but only because you have to make the patterns to fit your own chairs. The woodworking projects require skill with a variety of saws and a miter box. For all projects, read through the instructions carefully before buying materials.

antiqued bamboo headboard

(pages 30–31) Design: Sally Dixon

Materials

- Accordion-style bamboo garden trellis (from a garden shop or home center)
- Artist's oil paints: ivory black, burnt umber, yellow ocher
- Artist's linseed oil
- Plastic paint palette or disposable plastic plate
- Natural-bristle brushes
- Clear lacquer or oil-base spray varnish

Instructions

1. Protect your work surface with newspapers or an old shower curtain liner. Open the trellis fully. It will be easier to paint the trellis if you can lean it against a porch railing while you work on it. Cover the railing to protect it from paint.

2. Mix 2 parts burnt umber to 1 part ivory black and 1 part yellow ocher on the palette. Thin the paint with linseed oil until it's about the consistency of chocolate sauce—if it's too thick, the paint will be too opaque, but if it's as thin as the consistency of cream, it will be too translucent and runny. Because the bamboo is smooth, the paint may be somewhat streaky when you apply it, allowing the bamboo to show through.

3. Brush the paint onto the bamboo, covering both sides of the trellis. Keep the brush stokes vertical to simulate the "grain" of the bamboo.

4. Allow the paint to set for a few minutes, then drag a dry brush over the bamboo to remove some of the paint, creating the antiqued effect.

5. Let the paint dry completely (this could take about a week). Seal the surface with clear lacquer or oil-base polyurethane varnish. Mount on the wall with nails.

Above Squeeze about a tablespoon of each color onto the palette, then mix umber, black, and ocher in a ratio of 2:1:1. **Below** Brush the thinned paint onto both sides of the trellis.

china cabinet makeover

(page 118) Design: Deborah Hastings

Materials

³/₈-inch-thick foam-core board
Utility knife with new blades
Quilt batting
Masking tape
Fabric
Double-stick carpet tape (optional)

Instructions

1. Measure the height and width of the inside back of the china cabinet between the top shelf and the inside top of the cabinet. Repeat to measure between each shelf. You'll make a separate fabric-covered backing board for each section. Cut the foam-core to these measurements.

2. For each piece of foam-core board, cut batting 3 inches larger all around than the board. Center the foam-core on the batting and wrap the excess to the back. Secure the batting to the foam-core with masking tape.

3. For each piece of foam-core board, cut fabric to the same size as the batting. Center the batting-wrapped board on the wrong side of the fabric (batting side down) and pull the excess fabric to the back of the foam-core. Pull the fabric taut so the front is smooth and straight. Secure the fabric to the back of the foam-core board with masking tape.

4. Wedge the board in place at the back of the china cabinet. It should fit snugly. If necessary, use small pieces of double-stick carpet tape to hold the board in place.

chair skirt slipcovers

(page 120) Design: Deborah
 Hastings

Materials

Tape measure
Sheer drapery fabric (see instructions
 for yardage calculations)
Thread to match fabric
Sewing machine
$5/8$-inch fusible bonding tape
$1/4$-inch-wide organza ribbon

instructions

1. To calculate yardage requirements,
   measure one chair as follows, then
   multiply by the number of chairs you'll
   be slipcovering. Most upholstery and
   drapery fabrics are 54 inches wide.

2. For the seat cover, measure the seat's
   width and length and add $1/2$ inch all
   around for seam allowances. Draw a
   paper pattern to these dimensions.

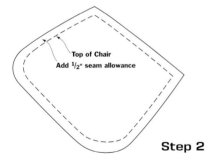

Top of Chair
Add $1/2$" seam allowance

Step 2

3. For the skirt side and front panel,
   measure around the seat from stile to
   stile (the posts that form the chair
   back) and add 12 inches to gather the
   fabric at the front corners; also add
   twice the width of the back chair leg
   and add 1 inch for seam allowances.

177

For the drop, measure from the seat to the floor and add 3$\frac{1}{2}$ inches for hem and seam allowances. Cut the required number of panels to these measurements. Cut the back edge of the skirt to match the angle of the back chair leg. You may need to piece fabric widths to obtain the required panel length. (For the skirt back panel, see step 7.)

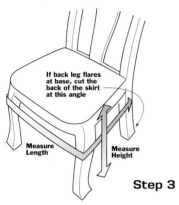

Step 3

4. Use the paper pattern for the seat cover to cut the required number of covers. Finish the back edge of each with a princess seam (double-fold the raw edge as narrowly as possible and stitch). Set the seat covers aside.

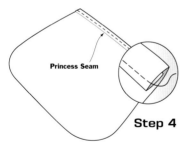

Princess Seam

Step 4

5. To hem the skirt, fold the lower 3 inches to the front (right side of the fabric) and secure the raw edge to the fabric using fusible bonding tape and organza ribbon (see diagram).

6. Starting at one short end of the skirt, mark a $\frac{1}{2}$-inch seam allowance, the width of the back chair leg, and the length of one side of the chair

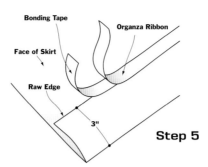

Bonding Tape
Organza Ribbon
Face of Skirt
Raw Edge
3"

Step 5

seat. Mark this point, then measure 6 inches and mark. Mark the measurement of the chair seat front, then measure 6 inches and mark. Using a long stitch length, make two rows of gathering stitches in the two 6-inch areas. Pull up the bobbin threads to gather, fitting the skirt to the chair seat (see diagram). Stitch the skirt panel to the seat cover, allowing the short ends to extend beyond the back edge of the seat by the width of the chair leg and the seam allowance (see diagram).

Step 6

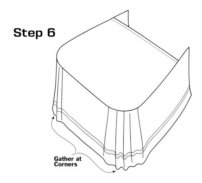

Gather at Corners

7. For the skirt back panel, measure from the outside edge of each back leg to the center back; add 3 inches for overlap plus $\frac{1}{2}$-inch seam allowances on the side and top edges and 3 inches for the hem. Cut two pieces of fabric to these measurements.

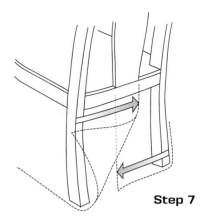

Step 7

8. Fold and iron the hem as directed in step 5. Stitch the back sections to the front and side panel (see diagram). Finish the raw edges with princess seams. Stitch a 20-inch length of organza ribbon to the top outside edge of each back skirt piece.

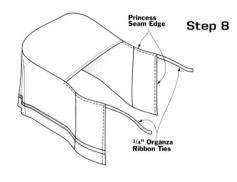

Princess Seam Edge   **Step 8**

$\frac{1}{4}$" Organza Ribbon Ties

9. To tie the skirt onto the chair, wrap the ties around the center back of the chair and tie at the back.

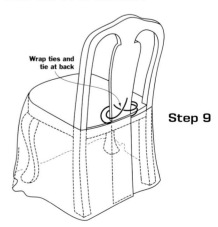

Wrap ties and tie at back

Step 9

10. For armchairs, measure from arm to arm around the chair seat; add 12 inches for gathering, plus 1 inch for seam allowances. Cut separate panels for the sides, measuring from in front of the arm to the back of the back leg, allowing for overlap with the front skirt. Make the back panels as directed in steps 7 and 8. Hem as directed in step 5. Finish the raw edges with princess seams; use hook-and-loop dots at the top and bottom edges to secure (see diagram below).

Step 10

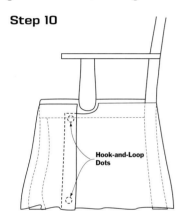

Hook-and-Loop Dots

marble-top sideboard
(page 121) Design: Deborah Hastings

Materials
Narrow wrought-iron table
5/8-inch plywood
Marble tiles (from a home center)
Basecap or molded trim wide enough to cover the raw edge of the plywood and the edge of the tiles
Circular saw, miter saw
Finish nails and wood screws
Paint to match the marble

Instructions

1. The marble tiles should be wide enough to cover the top of the table or extend slightly beyond the edge of the table. Lay the tiles on the plywood, butting them together tightly (see diagram). Draw around the tiles on the plywood to mark the cutting line. Cut the top from the plywood.

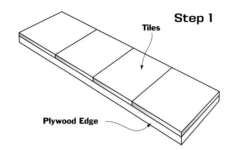

Step 1

Tiles

Plywood Edge

2. Cut the molding to fit the sides and front edge, mitering the corners. Nail the molding to the edges of the plywood. Paint the molding, then slide the tiles into place from the back. If the fit is snug, the tiles won't need to be grouted. Screw the plywood top to the table from below.

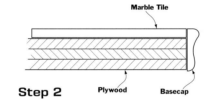

Marble Tile

Step 2   Plywood   Basecap

bed skirt
(page 128) Design: Linda Wright

Materials
54-inch-wide medium-weight upholstery fabric and lining (see steps 1 and 4 to calculate yardage)
Sewing machine
Thread to match fabric
Gathering tape (optional)
Upholstery pins (from a fabric store) or large safety pins

Instructions

1. For the depth of the skirt, measure the drop from the top of the box springs to the floor. Add $4\frac{1}{2}$ inches for hems and $\frac{1}{2}$-inch seam allowance. Cut three widths of 54-inch-wide fabric to this measurement for each side of the bed. Cut two widths for the foot of the bed (a total of eight pieces).

2. To make one side panel, stitch three widths together at the short ends. At each end of this panel, press under $\frac{1}{2}$ inch twice and stitch. Repeat this procedure to make the second side panel and the foot panel.

3. To hem each section, fold under 2 inches twice and press. Blindstitch the folded edge.

4. Measure the length and width of the box springs. Double the length measurement, add the width measurement, and cut a 6-inch-wide strip of lining equal to this sum. (You may have to piece strips to obtain the needed length.) Fold the strip in half lengthwise, wrong sides facing; press.

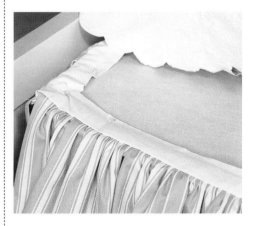

5. To gather the top (unfinished) edge of the skirt, use gathering tape or make two rows of long stitches in the seam allowance. Gather the side and foot panels to fit the length and width of

the box springs. Stitch the gathered panels to the raw edges of the lining strip, right sides facing and raw edges aligned. Stitch through both layers of lining. To secure the bed skirt to the box springs, push upholstery pins or safety pins through the lining tape.

duvet Cover

(page 128) Design: Linda Wright

Materials
54-inch-wide lightweight or medium
   weight upholstery fabric
54-inch-wide companion fabric
Threads to match fabrics
Sewing machine
Cording with lip and coordinating ribbon
1½-inch-diameter buttons to cover

instructions

1. Measure the comforter length and width. For the back of the cover, cut the primary fabric to this size plus ½ inch all around for seam allowances. (You may need to piece widths of fabric to achieve the desired cover width. If so, cut two panels to the required length, cut one panel in half lengthwise, and stitch one half to each side of the remaining panel.)

2. For the front of the cover, cut the companion fabric to measure the same width as the back but 10 inches shorter. From the primary fabric, cut a strip 24 inches wide and as long as the cover is wide. This will be the flap.

3. Turn under ½ inch at the top edge of the cover front and stitch. On the bottom edge of the flap, fold under 1½ inches twice and stitch close to the second fold. About 1 inch from the hemmed edge, make six to eight 1½-inch buttonholes evenly spaced across the flap's long edge.

4. Stitch cording to the right side of the cover back, aligning the edge of the lip with the raw edge of the fabric. In each corner, on the wrong side, stitch a 10-inch length of ribbon folded in half. Use this ribbon to tie the comforter in place inside the cover.

5. To assemble the cover, lay the cover back with the right side faceup. Place the flap right side facedown, aligning it with the top edge of the cover back. Place the cover front right side facedown, aligning it with the bottom edge of the cover back. Stitch around the outside edges using a ½-inch seam allowance.

6. Turn to the right side through the flap. Cover the buttons, following the manufacturer's instructions. Sew to the cover, lining the buttons up with the buttonholes. Press the finished cover. Insert the comforter. Tie the ribbons around each corner of the comforter to hold it in place.

neck roll pillow

(page 128) Design: Linda Wright

Materials
Lightweight or medium-weight
   upholstery fabric and two companion
   fabrics (for yardage, see instructions)
Thread to match fabrics
Decorative trim or braid (for yardage,
   see instructions)
Sewing machine
22-inch-long bolster form
Ribbon or cord

Instructions

1. Cut one 12×29-inch piece from the primary fabric for the center section. Cut two 5×29-inch side strips from one companion fabric. Cut two 5×29-inch end strips from the second companion fabric.

2. Stitch one side strip to each long edge of the center section, right sides facing and raw edges aligned. Stitch one end strip to the long edge of each side strip.

3. Stitch decorative trim or braid over the seams. Turn under $^3/_4$ inch on the long raw edge of each end piece and stitch close to the raw edge to hem.

4. With right sides facing, stitch the long raw edges of the pillow cover, forming a tube. Turn the tube to the right side. Insert the pillow form.

5. Remove some of the stitches in the $^3/_4$-inch hem at each end of the tube and insert cord or ribbon. Run the cord through the hem and pull tightly to gather the end. Knot the ribbon and tuck the excess ribbon ends inside the pillow cover.

Window Seat

(page 144) Design: Deborah Hastings and Linda Wright

Materials
2×4s (quantity will depend on space)
16d casing nails, 6d finish nails
Yellow carpenter's glue
1 sheet of $^3/_4$-inch birch plywood
Piano hinge, mending plates
Drill and drill bits
Saber saw, circular or hand saw
Paint to match wall (optional)

instructions

1. Measure your dormer to determine the size of the window seat. The one shown is 24 inches deep and 19 inches tall. If your house isn't absolutely square, measure the width of the dormer at the opening and again close to the window at 4 inches and 19 inches above the floor. Take the smaller width measurement and subtract ½ inch from it for the width of the window seat.

Step 1

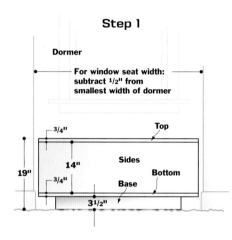

- Dormer
- For window seat width: subtract ½" from smallest width of dormer
- ¾" — Top
- Sides
- 19"
- 14"
- ¾" — Bottom
- Base
- 3½"

2. Cut and assemble the base from 2×4s as shown below, using butt joints. Secure with glue and nails. The base should measure 12 inches smaller in width and depth than the size of the box that makes up the seat. The base lifts the box above the baseboard so you don't have to make special cuts to fit the box snugly against the wall.

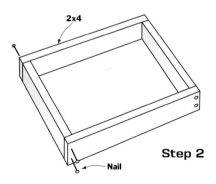

- 2×4
- Nail

Step 2

3. From plywood, cut the top and bottom of the seat box to the measured dimensions. Cut the sides to fit flush. The sides of the window seat shown measure 24 inches wide by 14 inches tall (19 inches minus the height of the 2×4 base—3½ inches—and the ¾-inch top and bottom panels).

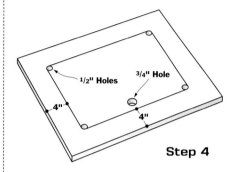

- ½" Holes
- ¾" Hole
- 4"
- 4"

Step 4

4. For the lid, measure in 4 inches from each side of the top piece and mark. Drill a ½-inch hole in each corner. Use these holes to insert the saw blade and cut out the lid. Drill a ¾-inch hole in the center front to lift the lid.

5. Screw four mending plates across the corners of the underside of the frame as shown.

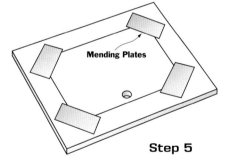

- Mending Plates

Step 5

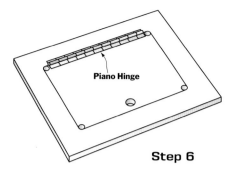

- Piano Hinge

Step 6

6. On the opposite side, attach the lid with the piano hinge.

7. Glue and nail the sides, front and back together; glue and nail with 6d finish nails the top and bottom, and attach the box to the 2×4 base. Paint the window seat to match the walls.

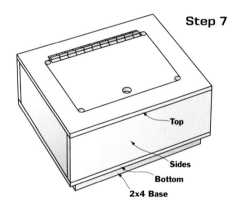

- Top
- Sides
- Bottom
- 2×4 Base

Step 7

8. To make the skirt, measure from the top of the seat to the floor and add 6 inches for hems. For the width, measure the width of the seat box and add 6 inches for the center pleat and 2 inches for side hems. Cut upholstery fabric to these measurements, then cut the panel in half. For the pleat insert, cut a strip of contrast fabric 7 inches wide and the same depth as the skirt. Sew the contrast strip to the panel halves, using a ½-inch seam allowance. Make a 3-inch-deep pleat on each side of the center, placing the seams in the

inside folds. Turn under the side edges of the panels ½ inch and hem. Cut a fabric strip 6 inches wide and ½ inch longer than the skirt width. Sew this strip across the top of the skirt, right sides facing, letting the strip extend ¼ inch beyond each end. Press under ¼ inch on each raw edge, then fold the strip in half and stitch. Use a staple gun to secure the strip to the plywood top. Make a box cushion, using a purchased pattern.

bench

(page 97) Design: Deborah Hastings

Materials

One 6-foot 1×10 pine board
Two 6-foot 1×4 pine boards
Two 2-foot 1×12 pine boards
Two 6-foot 1×2 pine boards
4d finish nails
Wood glue
Radial arm saw, saber saw, dovetail saw
Latex paint: flat red, flat black
Paste wax

instructions

1. The 1×10 is the seat. For the aprons, cut the 1×4s to 71 inches, mitering the ends 45 degrees as shown.

Step 1

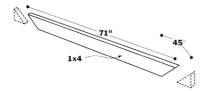

71"
45°
1x4

2. To attach the aprons, draw a line down the center of the 1×10 top, then measure and mark along the length 4⅛ inches from the center (about ⅝ inch from the edge on each side). Using glue and finish nails, attach the aprons, starting at the angled ends and working from the bottom. Turn the top over and finish nailing along the length of the board from the top into the aprons.

3. The legs of the bench angle at 15 degrees for greater stability. Cut 20-inch-long pieces from the 1×12s, angling the cuts 15 degrees as shown. Use a radial arm saw, tilting the blade 15 degrees, or use a saber saw with the base tilted to cut at 15 degrees.

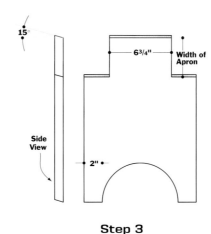

15°
6¾"
Width of Apron
Side View
2"

Step 3

4. To keep the bench from wobbling, cut a 4-inch-radius half-circle out of the bottom edge of each leg, using a dish

or lid as a template. Allow 2 inches on each side of the cutout. At the top, to receive the aprons, cut a notch from each top corner of each leg piece. The side cut will angle 15 degrees; to mark it, lay the apron board across the side at the 15 degree angle and mark. Use a dovetail saw to make the apron cuts and a saber saw for the bottom half-circle.

5. Place the apron in the notch and mark its outside edge on the face of the leg. Draw a line from this mark to the outside edge of the foot. Cut along this line to angle the leg.

Step 5

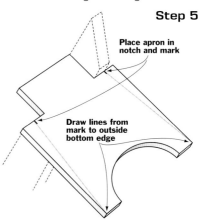

Place apron in notch and mark

Draw lines from mark to outside bottom edge

6. For the stretchers, place a 1×2 4½ inches from the bottom of the leg and mark the sides of the leg at 15 degrees. Use a sliding angle finder from a hardware store to mark the side cuts. Cut the notches with a saber saw.

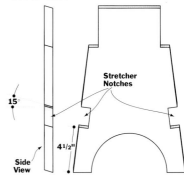

Stretcher Notches
15°
4½"
Side View

7. Attach the legs with wood glue and 4d finish nails, positioning them 10 inches in from each end.

Step 7

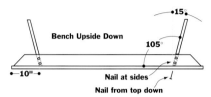

8. Slip the 1×2 stretchers into the notches and mark on the back where they need to be cut. Cut them to fit and glue and nail in place.

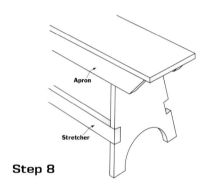

Step 8

9. For a rustic finish, do not prime the bench. Sand the edges so they look worn. Apply a red undercoat. Let the paint dry, then apply a black top coat. After the black dries, sand along edges and at any natural wear points to let some red show through. Apply a coat of wax for a subtle luster.

louvered screen

(page 163) Design: Deborah Hastings

Materials (for screen to fit over a tub with an 8-foot ceiling)
Three 6-foot 2×2 boards
Two 6-foot 1×4 boards
One 1×10×6 MDF board
Six 10-foot lengths of 2½-inch lath
Two 6-foot lengths of quarter-round trim
Radial arm saw
3-inch drywall screws, 2½-inch wood screws, 4d finish nails
Caulk, paint, paintbrush

instructions

1. The screen shown is 25 inches tall on a 20-inch frame. To determine the width for your tub and shower, measure the distance from wall to wall and subtract ½ inch. Cut two 2×2s to this measurement. Cut three 2×2s to 16½ inches.

2. To receive the lath strips, use a radial arm saw set at a 45-degree angle to cut grooves ¼ inch deep and 1½ inches apart in the three 16½-inch 2×2s (see diagram). Make sure the grooves are perfectly aligned and wide enough to receive the edge of the lath. Make the fit a little loose; paint will add thickness. Assemble the 2×2s as shown in the diagram, using wood glue and wood screws. Cut the lath to fit the grooves.

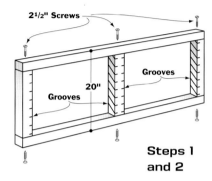

Steps 1 and 2

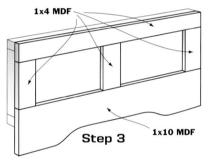

Step 3

3. For the facing, cut the 1×4s and the 1×10 MDF to fit the measured space (see the diagram). (MDF will give a smoother finish.) Glue and nail in place with 4-penny nails. Prime the piece.

4. Using the 3-inch drywall screws, mount the frame to the wall and ceiling above the tub.

5. Cover the gaps at the sides with quarter-round molding. Caulk the seams and paint the frame. Prime and paint the lath strips and slip them into place from the back.

mosaic mirror

(page 162) Design: Deborah Hastings

Materials
¹⁄₄-inch plywood
Circular or saber saw
Caulk
Liquid Nails or 4d finish nails
Clear acrylic adhesive caulk
Silver paint, paint brush
Thick white crafts glue and tiny nails
Assorted seashells
1×1-inch glass tiles in assorted colors

instructions

1. Using ¹⁄₄-inch-thick plywood (or plywood the same thickness as the mirror), cut a decorative pediment that extends above the light fixture. Cut an opening for the fixture. Nail the board to the wall. Caulk the seam between the top of the mirror and the plywood and around the light fixture. Paint the plywood silver.

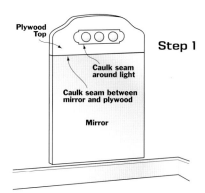

Step 1

Plywood Top

Caulk seam around light

Caulk seam between mirror and plywood

Mirror

2. Begin gluing shells to the top of the pediment, using a large featured shell in the center. To secure heavier shells, hang them over tiny nails as well as gluing them. Glue shells along the top curved edge until the pediment is covered.

Feature Shell

Step 2

3. Remove the 1-inch-square tiles from the paper backing by soaking them in water. Glue the tiles to the mirror using clear acrylic adhesive caulk. Butt the tiles together to eliminate the need for grout. Attach a border of four rows of tiles along the bottom of the mirror, then build up the sides with

rows of four tiles, working all the way up to the pediment. Trim tiles as necessary to fit around the light fixture and the edges of the shells.

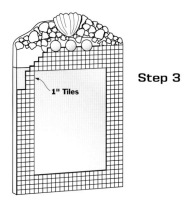

Step 3

1" Tiles

cabinet doors

(page 162) Design: Deborah Hastings

1. Using screen lath, mark an X on the flat panels of the cabinet doors.

2. Cut one strip to fit diagonally across the panels. Mark where it meets the routed edges and cut at an angle with a coping saw.

3. Repeat for the opposite side, but cut in the center to cross the first strip. Glue the strips in place. Caulk the gaps and paint to match the cabinet.

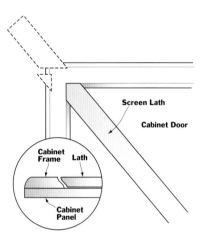

Screen Lath

Cabinet Door

Cabinet Frame   Lath

Cabinet Panel

Step 2

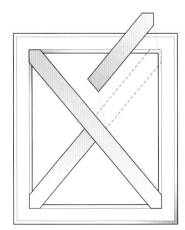

Step 3

daybed frame

(page 161) Design: Deborah Hastings

Materials

Two 6-foot 2×6 knot-free boards (such as poplar, fir, or birch)
28 dowels ³/₄ inch in diameter and 48 inches long
One 8-foot 1×8 board
Table or circular saw
6d finish nails, yellow carpenter's glue
Metal frame for a daybed

1. Cut the 2×6s into four 36-inch lengths. Draw a 5¹/₂-inch-diameter circle at one end of each for a rounded top. (The straight bottoms will be 4 inches wide.) Mark each board as shown and cut away the gray area with a table saw or circular handsaw.

Step 1

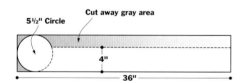

5¹/₂" Circle
Cut away gray area
4"
36"

2. Measure 14 inches from the bottom of each leg and mark on each side the width and depth of the 1×8 (see the diagram below). Use a scrap of 1×8, set it on end on the leg, and draw around it for the cutout. Cut out this section from each leg.

Step 2

14"

3. To determine the length of the dowels, measure the depth of the metal bed frame, subtract the combined width of the two legs, and add 2 inches (¹/₂ inch for the depth that the dowel will sink into each leg and ¹/₂ inch to accommodate the bed frame front and back).

4. Make a template for drilling the holes for the dowels and mark the legs. Be sure to align them so the holes will be drilled on the correct side of each leg.

Step 4

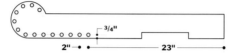

3/4"
2"
23"

5. To drill the holes exactly ¹/₂ inch deep, use a drill press or an attachment on your portable drill that will keep the depth consistent and the drill perpendicular to the surface.

6. To cut the 1×8 lower panels the correct length, measure the depth of the metal frame and add 1 inch. Cut two. Place a drop of glue in each dowel hole and on the notched areas of one front and back leg. Place the dowels in the holes (this may require two people). Place the 1×8 in the notches, keeping the ends flush with the outside front and back legs. Nail in place to hold until the glue dries.

7. Repeat for the remaining side. When the glue dries, sand and prime the wood and paint.

8. Bolt the metal frame to the 1×8 cross pieces, positioning the top of the frame 17 inches from the floor. This leaves clearance for a trundle bed underneath.

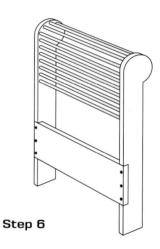

Step 6

187

barstool slipcovers

(page 153) Design: Catheryn Wilson, ASID)

1. Wash cotton fabric before cutting to prevent shrinkage during cleaning. Use lightweight to mediumweight upholstery fabric; if the fabric is thin enough to allow the original upholstery to show through, you'll need to line the slipcover pieces before assembling. Use paper to make a pattern of the back of the barstool, adding a $\frac{1}{2}$-inch seam allowance. Cut a front and back from fabric. Pin to mark where the chair back meets the arm. With right sides facing, stitch the front and back along the top between the pins. Stitch hook-and-loop tape to the side and bottom edges.

2. For the chair seat, use paper or muslin to make a pattern. Cut openings to fit around the arm posts and stiles. Add $\frac{1}{2}$ inch to all cut edges for hemming. Cut the pattern from fabric. Hem the raw edges by turning them under $\frac{1}{4}$ inch twice and topstitching close to the fold.

3. For ties, cut eight 2×6-inch strips of fabric. Fold each strip in half lengthwise and stitch all raw edges, leaving an opening for turning. Turn, stitch the opening closed, and pin one tie to the wrong side of the seat cover at the edge of each opening. Topstitch in place. Tie the seat cover in place with square knots and tuck the ends under the cover.

folding screen

(page 23) Design: Deborah Hastings

Materials

Two pairs of unfinished wood raised-
    panel bifold doors
Two $1/2$-inch-wide 2-inch hinges
One 2-foot 1×2 pine or fir board
Yellow carpenter's glue
6d finish nails
Drill and drill bits
One quart red semigloss latex paint
One quart black semigloss latex paint
Paintbrushes
Crackle medium
Medium and coarse sandpaper
Paste wax

instructions

1. Using the two hinges, attach the pairs
   of doors to create a four-panel
   screen. Cut the 1×2 board into eight
   $2^{1}/_{2}$-inch lengths. These will be
   attached to the bottom of each panel
   to add stability. Cut away one side on
   a curve for a decorative effect, if
   desired.

2. Glue and nail the feet to each panel,
   using finish nails. (Drill small pilot holes
   before nailing to prevent splitting the
   wood.)

3. Paint the door panels red and let dry.
   Brush crackle medium over the piece
   in patches. When the medium is tacky,
   apply black paint to the entire screen.
   Let the paint dry.

4. To add "weathering," rub along the
   edges with coarse, and then medium,
   sandpaper. Seal with several coats of
   paste wax.

Index

* resources

manufacturers

Benjamin Moore Paints: Call 800/672-4686 to find a local dealer, or visit the website at benjaminmoore.com.

Crate and Barrel: 800/451-8217

Ethan Allen, Inc.: 800/228-9229

Garnet Hill Catalog: 800/622-6216; garnethill.com

Hunter Douglas Window Fashions: 800/937-7895; hunterdouglas.com.

IKEA: 800/434-4532; ikea-usa.com.

Laura Ashley: For nearest shop, call 800/367-2000.

Pier 1 Imports, Inc., For store locations, call 800/447-4371; pier1.com

Pottery Barn: 800/922-5507.

Restoration Hardware: 888/243-9720; restorationhardware.com

Room and Board: Call 800/486-6554 for a catalog or visit online roomandboard.com.

Simon Pearce: 800/774-5277; simonpearce.com.

Shaker Workshops: 800/840-9121; shakerworkshops.com.

Pages 8–13
Interior design: Sandy Lucas, ASID; Lucas/Eilers Design Assoc., 1502 Augusta, #220, Houston, TX 77057; 713/784-9423. Painted fish plates: Mary Thyssen, Designs for Tiles, 1907 Old Colony Court, Richmond, TX 77469; 281/341-9002 .

Pages 14–17
Qbits stackable storage by Lynnette Jennings available at Target and home centers.

Pages 18–19, 91, 154
Interior design: Kitty Starling, IADA, Incredible Interiors, 327 Seminole Drive, Marietta, GA 30060; 770/794-1972; kitstar@mindspring.com. For information about the Interior Arrangement and Design Association (IADA), write to IADA, Box 777, 6333 East Mockingbird, Suite 147, Dallas, TX 75214-2692; 214/826-2474. Or visit the website at interiorarrangement.org

Pages 26–31, 38–41, 122–123, 155
Interior design: Sally Dixon, Dixon & Martin Building and Interior Design, 3639 Charles St., San Diego, CA 92106; 619/225-1668; sallydixon@cox.net

Pages 36–37, 74–87, 104–109
Interior design: Kitty Starling, IADA, and Donna Mobley, IADA. To contact Kitty Starling, see under Pages 18–19. To contact Donna Mobley, Donna Mobley Designs, call 912/897-6310 or e-mail iadasav@earthlink.net.

Pages 42–43
Interior design: Lisa Billings, IADA, and Susie Ingram, IADA; to contact IADA members, see under Pages 18–19. Butterfly chairs, pillows: Crate and Barrel.

Pages 44–47
Leather rug, taller coffee table, picture chain in playroom: IKEA. Book table: Target. Leather chairs, ottoman, sofa: Pottery Barn.

Pages 50–57, 116–117
Interior Design: Susan Andrews, 5440 West 101st Terr., Overland Park, KS 66207. Paint: Benjamin Moore; living room, Princeton Gold; fireplace, Sangria; dining room, Livingston Gold; entry, Split Pea. Artwork on dining room fireplace, Tina Blanck. Furniture: Room & Board; living room: 60-inch Nelson Bench, Ebony; wood armchairs, Pearson/natural; armoire, Linear/maple; end tables with stainless steel tops; by fireplace, chair and ottoman Jasper/Cement; by dining room fireplace: chairs Neal/Mars Crimson. Window treatment: Pottery Barn. Square/round chair: Bergamot & Ivy, Kansas City, MO; 816/561-5599. Retro lamps in entry: Retro Inferno, 1712 Main, Kansas City, MO; 816/842-4004.

Pages 70–73
Interior design: Lisa Billings, IADA, and Susie Ingram, IADA. Dining room table and chairs, living room sofa, coffee table, leather chair and ottoman: Ethan Allen, Inc. Dining room candlesticks, vase, rug, table runner (two curtain panels), living room fireplace screen, pillows, red beaded floor lamp, throw: Pottery Barn.

Pages 88–89
Wallpaper in "after": Seabrook. Call 800/238-9152 for local retailer.

Pages 94–99
Rattan armchairs, basket on coffee table, rug: Pottery Barn. Table between chair, mantel vases: At Home, Homewood, AL. Wrought iron, mantel, stairwell: Tricia's Treasures, Vestavia, AL; 205/822-0004. Mantel candlesticks, dining table cloth, urn with bamboo sticks, sunroom iron plant stand, bedside and dresser lamps: Pier 1. Lamp on table between chairs: Restoration Hardware. China: Vietri, through The China Closet, Vestavia, AL. Print over sideboard: Harmony Landing, Homewood, Ala. Sunroom wicker chair: Drexel Heritage through Fine Furniture, Vestavia, AL. Bedroom picture frames: Michael's Stores.

Pages 118–121
Slipcover fabric, seat covers, table runner: Calico Corners. China cabinet fabric: Fabric Jungle. Draperies: Pottery Barn. Iron table: Fontera, Birmingham, AL. Lamps: Lowe's. China: Lennox "Solitaire."

Pages 128–131
Fabrics: Garden Toile/Apple, Colwyn/Rose by Braemoor. End tables, white lamp, Pottery Barn. Linens, transferware paper plates, Christine's, Mountain Brook, AL.

Pages 132–137
Produced by Tricia Foley. Top coverlet, The Garnet Hill Catalog. Shutters: Lantana white, specially engineered polymer, Palm Beach Custom collection, Hunter Douglas Window Fashions. Lamp: Simon Pearce. Bench: Shaker Workshops. Rug: Buckingham Jute, oatmeal, Import Specialists, 800/334-4044. Wall paint: Benjamin Moore #2018-60 Lighthouse; 800/826-2623. Upholstered rocker: Restoration Hardware. Raffia-wrapped storage boxes in armoire: Crate and Barrel. Shower curtain, sink skirt fabric: Falmouth Check, cowslip, Laura Ashley. Étagère: Los Gatos, Ernest Hemingway collection, Thomasville Furniture. Wall paint: Benjamin Moore #HC-4 Hawthorne Yellow. Dresser: Nellie Six-Drawer, Maine Cottage Furniture, 207/846-1430; mainecottage.com. Magazine files: IKEA.

Pages 138–141
Interior designer: Sandy Lucas, ASID; see under Pages 8–13. Boys' room: striped rug, "4-Spangled Banner," The Great Rug Co., Houston, Tex.; 713/789-3666. Pond yacht, Susan Bragg Antiques, Houston, Tex.; 713/520-9755. Quilts, Chenielle Stars airplanes and stars pillows, Land of Nod catalog, 800/933-9904.

Page 144
Window treatments: Pate Meadows, Birmingham, Ala., 205/823-7953.

Pages 146–153
Interior design: Catheryn Wilson, ASID, 1803 Bradmore, Houston, TX 77077; 281/493-9330. Linen square pillows (summer) by Ann Gish, botanical prints, red square wool tablecloth, shaped wooden platter (winter), from Kuhl-Linscomb, 2424 W. Alabama, Houston, TX 77098; 713/526-6000. Spode "Pink Tower" dinner plates (winter), Bering's, 3900 Bissonnet, Houston, TX 77005. Slipcover fabrics, Kravet Collection.

Pages 160–163
Draperies: Pottery Barn. Vase on table: Restoration Hardware. Curtain rods: Target. Pillows: Pier 1, Target, Wal-Mart. Fabric for daybed skirt: Waverly. Tray table: Harmony Landing, 2925 18th St., Birmingham, AL 35209; 205/871-0585. Mirror tiles: Ann Sacks manufacturer. Curtain fabric: Waverly. Rug: T.J. Maxx.

Pages 164–169
Design: Patricia Hansen. Wall paint Ralph Lauren River Rock Collection, "Old Holland Warm Gray."

Pages 170–173
Architectural artifacts and birdhouses: Donna Bokland, Ecclectica Homewares, 518/869-9914. Decorative painting on walls: Anita Medina, Carnelian, 5A Ledgewood Dr., Albany, NY 12205; 518/458-9240.